TAXES, BENEF
FAMILY LIFE:

The Seven Deadly Traps

HERMIONE PARKER

Published by
INSTITUTE OF ECONOMIC AFFAIRS
1995

First published August 1995 by

The Institute of Economic Affairs,
2 Lord North Street,
Westminster, London SW1P 3LB

Research Monograph No.50 constitutes the revised and extended Second Edition of Research Monograph No.37, *The Moral Hazard of Social Benefits*, first published by the IEA in October 1982.

ISSN 0073-9103
ISBN 0-255 36370-2

Typography by Stuart Blade Enterprises

Cover design by David Lucas

Printed in Great Britain by
Bourne Press, Bournemouth, Dorset
Set in Univers 9 on 11 pt

Contents

LIST OF FIGURES

Foreword

In 1982, the Institute published Hermione Parker's *The Moral Hazard of Social Benefits* (Research Monograph No. 37) which discussed how the tax and benefit systems combine to produce disincentives to effort. Many changes have occurred to both systems in the last 13 years, along the same piecemeal lines criticised by Mrs Parker in 1982. Thus it seemed time to examine once more the consequences – intended and unintended – of the well-meaning efforts of politicians and civil servants to provide a social 'safety net'.

It is common enough to identify one or more 'traps' which result from the tax and benefit systems. But Mrs Parker's careful research and detailed analysis reveal no less than seven traps which produce serious disincentives to effort. Moreover, in her view, there are spillover effects which adversely affect family life:

> '... the traditional family, where the mother puts the children first and the father is the breadwinner, suffers from tax and benefit policies which undermine its financial independence during the crucial child-bearing and child-rearing years' (p.122).

Social security spending is, she believes, 'out of control' and 'the residual welfare state is turning into a disaster'. Most at fault are the policy-makers, not the claimants. There are perverse incentives which induce people '...to try to move themselves into the categories in which they know benefits will be available' (p.125). Consequently, enterprise is diverted from productive activities into playing a system established by the state.

But Mrs Parker is not concerned only with analysing the faults of the present régime. Her powerful critique leads her to propose a radically different alternative which, as she shows, has an impressive pedigree. Her suggestion for a social safety net is that each citizen should receive a 'basic income' in the form of a fixed-amount tax credit which would convert automatically into cash for those without income to set against it. She would start by converting personal income tax allowances and child credit into 'transitional basic income' of £20 a week for adults and £15·65 for children.

In all Institute publications, the views expressed are those of the author not the IEA (which has no corporate view), its Trustees, Directors or Advisers. Mrs Parker's *Research Monograph* is published as a thorough analysis of one of the most serious issues facing the government, and a stimulating contribution to ideas for resolving the crisis afflicting state welfare.

July 1995

COLIN ROBINSON
Editorial Director, Institute of Economic Affairs;
Professor of Economics, University of Surrey

The Author

HERMIONE PARKER is a freelance political economist and writer specialising in income redistribution and its effects on living standards, incentives, unemployment and family life. Educated at the University of St Andrews, where she gained a First Class Honours Degree in Political Economy and Modern History, she has been a research assistant at the House of Commons since 1972. Specialist Adviser to the Treasury and Civil Service Select Committee Sub-Committee on 'Enquiry into the Structure of Personal Income Taxation and Income Support' (1982-83). Member of the European Institute of Social Security since 1985. Academic Visitor at the London School of Economics (1984-87). Member of the Microsimulation Unit Advisory Group, Department of Applied Economics, University of Cambridge, since 1993. In 1984, she helped to form the Basic Income Research Group (now called the Citizen's Income Trust) and is editor of the *Citizen's Income Bulletin*. In 1986 she also helped to form the Family Budget Unit, and is presently its Director. Her published works include *The Moral Hazard of Social Benefits* (Research Monograph No.37, IEA, 1982), *Action on Welfare* (Social Affairs Unit, 1984), *Instead of the Dole: An enquiry into integration of the tax and benefit systems* (Routledge, 1989), *Child Tax Allowances? A comparison of child benefit, child tax reliefs, and basic incomes as instruments of family policy* (STICERD, London School of Economics, 1991).

Acknowledgements

My thanks are due to the many people who have commented upon or assisted with parts of the text, especially Age Concern, Professor A.B. Atkinson, Christopher Monckton and Holly Sutherland. Without Holly Sutherland's modelling expertise my analysis of the basic income reform option would not have been possible. I am also indebted to Gresham College for their support and interest, which included a seminar at Barnard's Inn Hall in February 1995; to the Nigel Vinson Charitable Trust; and most of all to the Institute of Economic Affairs for their interest and publication skills. Needless to say, any errors are entirely my own.

H.P.

Author's Introduction

Killing the Goose...

This study is concerned with the effects of Britain's tax and benefit systems on incentives to work and to save, and their impact on family life. It starts from the premise that men and women work primarily for financial gain. It accuses nobody of being 'work-shy' or 'scrounging'. It does not question the desirability of a social security safety net. Nor does it make judgements about lone parents. It aims only to show that the piecemeal growth of the post-war 'Beveridge' system of social security, combined with increasing dependence on means-tested benefits and a regressive tax system, are undermining the natural instincts of self-reliance and self-advancement, instead of harnessing them to the common good. *In short, government is killing the goose that lays the golden eggs.*

In 1993, I was invited by the Institute of Economic Affairs to update the findings of an earlier IEA Research Monograph (No.37), *The Moral Hazard of Social Benefits*, published in 1982. On re-reading the first edition after a gap of 11 years, I was immediately struck by how little it had achieved. In 1982, I had concluded that the chief cause of disincentives was not over-generous out-of-work benefits but excessive taxation of the lower paid, especially families with children:

> 'Income maintenance today is no longer simply a matter of how much is paid out by the state in welfare benefits. What the state takes away in taxation is equally important. This is a development of the utmost significance. But government is still conducted as though there had been no such change.'[1]

Today, government is still conducted as though nothing had changed. Yet the scale of the problem is larger and is set to become larger still. First, the lower paid (including disproportionate numbers of families with children) are charged income tax, national insurance (NI) contribution and council tax on earnings below the guaranteed amounts payable on income support (Britain's minimum income guarantee for the out-of-work). Then they are expected to claim all or part of their tax back through an assortment of means-tested benefits that have been carefully honed to exclude small savers, involve loss of privacy and require endless red tape. Claimants who

---

[1]   Hermione Parker, *The Moral Hazard of Social Benefits*, IEA Research Monograph No.37, London: Institute of Economic Affairs, 1982, p.109.

prefer to remain on the dole until they can find jobs that give them economic independence, are castigated for being feckless and workshy.

Gradually, as my research progressed and the scale of the tax increases since 1982 became apparent, I wondered how a government so strongly committed to a philosophy of strong families and self-reliance could introduce policy after policy which were bound to engender the opposite effects. The underlying reason appears to be incoherent policy-making, some of it dogma driven and some the result of a Treasury that does not move with the times. The scale of the problem is such that low unemployment is no longer compatible with sustainable economic growth. The labour market is polarising between two-earner and no-earner families, while at the bottom of the earnings distribution – and higher up it for families with children – there is a well of potential wage claims that will nip growth in the bud.

Reform must be interdepartmental and must start in the Treasury. Several options are available. My preferred option would entail partial integration of the tax and benefit systems, combining a universal basic income (BI) with an income-tested housing benefit. At first the Treasury would hate it, because they would have to change their accounting techniques. Later, as revenues began to accumulate and benefit expenditure stabilised, they might actually come to like it.

Terminology

Unavoidably, my text is full of technical terms. Most are explained in the Glossary (below, pp.137-145). During the past few years, a predilection on the part of government for euphemisms and the constant introduction of new terms for what are essentially the same benefits has added greatly to public confusion about the benefit system. Until 1988 social security benefits could be slotted into four main categories: universal, contributory, income-tested and means-tested. Supplementary benefit was means-tested, while family income supplement, housing benefit and rate rebates were income-tested. Since 1988 their equivalents are all means-tested, that is to say, they all involve a test of capital as well as income. Yet, for some unexplained reason, they are referred to by government as *income-related*. This terminology is so confusing that, for the purposes of this *Research Monograph*, the older terminology is retained.

Computer modelling

The computer modelling reported in Part 5 was carried out using POLIMOD, a progamme written by Holly Sutherland, as part of her research on policy simulation at the Microsimulation Unit, University of Cambridge. POLIMOD uses data from the Family Expenditure Survey, made available by the CSO through the ESRC Data Archive. Neither the CSO nor the Data Archive bears any responsibility for the analysis or interpretation of the data reported here.

June 1995   **HERMIONE PARKER**

PART ONE

The Problem Revisited

---

1. THE TAX-BENEFIT BALANCE

By their nature, all income support programmes jeopardise work incentives, because they narrow the gap between incomes in and out of a job. Yet it is economically desirable that work should always be financially attractive, not least for the lower paid, and that extra effort and skills should be rewarded. If even a small minority of the workforce is encouraged to draw unemployment benefit, invalidity benefit, income support, family credit or housing benefit when they could be financially self-supporting, or when they could be training to improve their marketable skills, then social security becomes an engine of impoverishment instead of a means to prevent poverty.

That every increase in the social security budget must be paid for out of taxes is obvious. It is less obvious that every rise in income tax, national insurance (NI) contributions and (especially) council tax can reduce still further the advantages of working. When rents, fares to work and pay policies involving 'wage restraint' are added in, the net financial advantages of working can be eliminated at the bottom of the earnings scale for single people and much higher up it for families with children.

Even with low benefit rates the incentive to work may still be weak if the rewards (after tax) from paid work are also low. The dilemma is best grasped in terms of a pair of scales with, on one side, out-of-work living standards (a function of benefit levels), and on the other in-work living standards (a function of wages net of direct taxation, housing costs, council tax and work expenses). To preserve work incentives the second scale must always be heavier than the first. The balance will tilt in favour of not working if benefits are raised or taxes increased, and markedly so if both occur together. One reason for increased welfare dependency since 1979, despite a string of benefit cuts, is the growing incidence of tax at the bottom of the earnings distribution.

Broadly speaking, neither the benefit changes nor the income tax cuts of the 1980s and early 1990s have improved work incentives at the bottom of the earnings distribution, because they have been offset by higher national insurance contributions, higher local taxes,[1]

---

[1] Local authority domestic rates were replaced by community charge in 1990 and by council tax in 1993. To avoid repetition, the term 'local authority taxes' will be used as a generic for all three.

colossal rent increases and an unprecedented switch to owner-occupation by families who cannot really afford it. For parents the scale of the problem has been multiplied by the freezing of child benefit between 1987 and 1991, the post-1991 targeting of child benefit on families with only one child, and reductions in the married couple's income tax allowance since 1992.

Within the benefit system the disincentive effects of different programmes vary according to the detail of the regulations. Some of the most powerful disincentives – red tape, for example – are regularly omitted from academic and other studies, because they cannot be quantified. At one end of the incentive scale are work-hostile programmes like income support (work-tested and means-tested) to receive which claimants must satisfy the authorities that they are out of work but available for work, on a low income and with savings of less than £3,000. At the other end of the scale are work-friendly programmes like child benefit (universal, tax-free, payable in or out of work) on which parents can build through paid work without form-filling or fear of prosecution. Although universal provision like child benefit looks extravagant, there may be long-term advantages from programmes that promote strong families and encourage people with low earnings potential to earn and to save. Unfortunately, the immediate revenue costs are easier to measure than the long-term advantages.

The balance upset

The danger is that once the balance between taxation and benefits is upset the process of increasing disincentives becomes cumulative. The stronger the relative attraction of benefits the larger will be the number of claimants, and the higher the tax falling on diminishing numbers of taxpayers. At first, the effects may be hardly noticeable, but gradually the rate of sustainable economic growth falls and the tax base is eroded. For as workers try to recoup their tax 'losses', there is pressure for increased wages which in turn leads to more unemployment, more spending on benefits and still higher taxes. Resources available for people in need are diminished, and there is a real possibility of generally falling living standards, with those least able to protect themselves the worst affected. In Britain taxes have been increasing faster than prices and earnings at least since the 1960s, and the fastest growers have been national insurance contributions and local authority taxes, which affect the lower-paid disproportionately. *Until this trend is reversed, the problem of unemployment will remain avoidably stubborn.*

Vacancies for the skilled

If the net reward for paid work compares unfavourably with the total package of benefits during unemployment or sickness, job vacancies at the lower end of the earnings scale become hard to fill and harder still to keep filled. The only people likely to accept them will be young single people and second earners – usually married women – and the women will probably quit if their husbands are made redundant, because wives' earnings reduce husbands' income support giros. Underlying unemployment will increase, reflecting partly migration to the black economy, partly the lengthening period of search as workers try to find jobs that are financially worthwhile, and partly the response by employers to the resulting upward pressures on pay. Inevitably the switch away from labour-intensive towards capital-intensive production will intensify. The consequent unemployment will be worst for families with children, young people, people with disabilities and others whose earnings potential is low in relation to their out-of-work benefit entitlements. Demand for skilled labour may remain buoyant, but here too there is a problem, for the UK benefit system excludes trainees and students from entitlement to benefit; hence the well-known problem of shortages of skilled workers alongside high unemployment.

It is a complex situation, but the underlying principle is simple. Governments which disregard the basic laws of supply and demand *at any level of earnings* imperil the smooth running of the economy. During the 1980s big cuts were made in income tax at the top of the income distribution, but not at the bottom. Of course some people are prepared to work for little or no extra reward. Many unemployed people do voluntary work and would do more if the benefit system permitted it. But this does not alter the fundamental truth that every narrowing of the margin between living standards in and out of work (*the unemployment trap*) diminishes the effective demand for paid work, while every narrowing of spending power differentials from different levels of gross earnings (*the poverty trap*) reduces the supply of skilled labour.

Where it can be shown that the tax-benefit structure is likely to have such effects, it would be better to change it quickly, even if this requires root-and-branch reform. In practice, decades have been wasted, first in arguments about the scale of the problem and then in a series of benefit cuts most of which have been to no avail because they have been offset by higher tax and other levies on the lower paid. So long as this strategy continues, there will be a continuing increase in the 'natural' rate of unemployment.

2. WESTMINSTER OUT OF TOUCH

At grass roots level, the anomalies discussed in this paper are not seriously disputed. Anecdotal evidence is freely given and overwhelming. Structured interviews produce similar findings. As a result of labour market change, many of those whom others call 'scroungers' have difficulty in knowing whether they are employed, self-employed, unemployed or working on the side, such is the fluidity of the labour market in which they operate.[2]

In 1979 Margaret (now Lady) Thatcher's Government came to power pledged to restore work incentives; instead, over 4 million families now depend on income support, compared with 'only' 1·3 million who depended on supplementary benefit in 1978-79. For most of that period priority was rightly given to the control of inflation, but the erosion of work incentives is itself a root cause of wage inflation which causes price inflation when monetary policy is permissive and thus leads to increased unemployment when monetary policy is tightened. *So long as the predisposing causes of inflation and unemployment continue to be neglected, a lasting remedy will not be found. High unemployment may remove the symptoms of inflation, but they will re-emerge when economic expansion resumes.*

If work incentives at the bottom of the earnings distribution are to improve, the earnings levels at which tax becomes payable need to be raised sharply – especially for families with children. Reducing the starting rate of income tax is a less effective instrument than raising tax thresholds, and reducing or phasing out the married couple's allowance has negative effects. Without the married couple's allowance, the 1994-95 tax threshold for single-earner families would have been £66·25 a week, compared with income support (when out of work) of £71·70 plus rent or mortgage interest, plus council tax (in full) and passport benefits like free prescriptions. Since the adult rates of income support now (rightly) count as part of taxable income, will the Inland Revenue charge unemployed couples income tax on their income support?

Trickle-down has not worked

One theory is that, by focusing tax cuts on the rich, the extra wealth they create will increase everybody's living standards. But in practice it has not happened. Figure 1.1 shows a 62 per cent increase in average real incomes in the top tenth of the population between 1979 and 1990, compared with a 14 per cent *fall* at the bottom. Today there are increasing signs that this policy is administratively and electorally untenable. Administrative systems cannot distinguish between the 'deserving' and 'undeserving' poor on so large a scale, and there are electoral constraints to further benefit cuts. Whilst in 1982 supplementary benefit payments – with hidden extras and long-term additions – had become grossly inflated, by 1994 there was no fat left. That is why 63 per cent of

---

[2]   Bill Jordan, Simon James, Helen Kay and Marcus Redley, *Trapped in Poverty: Labour-Market Decisions in Low-Income Households*, London: Routledge, 1992.

FIGURE 1.1:
Changes in Income Distribution, 1979-90

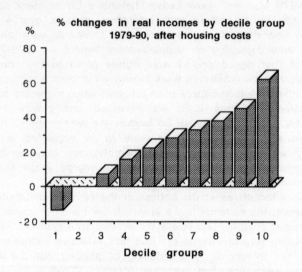

% changes in real incomes by decile group
1979-90, after housing costs

Source: Hansard, Written Answer, 18 October 1993, cols. 166-67.

respondents to the 1993 Social Attitudes Survey (including 55 per cent of Conservatives) favoured higher social benefits, compared with only 32 per cent (including 24 per cent of Conservative supporters) in 1983.[3]

3. FAMILY POLICY

Although the emphasis of this study is on work incentives, it is also concerned with family income support. Many of Britain's families are in a state of crisis. The days of the family wage are over. During the crucial child-rearing years both parents require paid work, unless one of them has above-average wages. Without two pay packets, many are better off on the dole. Britain is no longer a family-friendly country. Although successive governments make pro-family noises, their policies often appear family-hostile. In countries which set greater store on strong families, the purpose of family income support (tax reliefs and child benefits) is to smooth out the peaks and troughs of incomes and expenditure across the life cycle (without undermining family responsibility). In Britain, despite occasional high-sounding rhetoric in defence of the family, Government Ministers lack a clear understanding of family policy,

---

[3] Roger Jowell *et al.*, *British Social Attitudes*, the 11th Report, Social & Community Planning Research, 1994, p.3.

and have no generally accepted principles to guide them. During the 1970s there was talk of 'family impact statements', but it did not bear fruit. Many of today's social and economic problems – from work disincentives to family break up and (some would argue) the crime wave – result partly from this vacuum.

'Now that husbands and wives are taxed independently, married couple's allowance is a bit of an anomaly', said the Chancellor of the Exchequer in his 1993 Budget speech, before announcing cuts in the married couple's allowance. Lower income tax rates are being given priority over strong families. Insofar as married couple's allowance advantages two-earner couples, it is indeed anomalous. But to tax single-earner couples like single people would be even worse. Other options exist, such as *transferable income tax allowances* and *convertible tax credits/basic incomes.*[4]

The purpose of transferable income tax allowances is to enable the spouse without income (or with income smaller than the tax allowance) to transfer it (or the unused part of it) to the spouse with income. This system, or its equivalent, is used in many countries. In 1986 the Treasury ruled it out[5] on expense grounds, but its calculations excluded the long-term social security costs of reduced work incentives and family breakdown.

Transferable income tax allowances do, however, have disadvantages, for instance if the combined income of both spouses is less than their combined tax allowances and in cases where the spouse in work (usually the husband) 'hogs' both tax allowances (thereby discouraging his wife from taking paid work). Hence part of the case for convertible tax credits or basic incomes. With this option, all income tax allowances are replaced by income guarantees to which every legal resident is entitled, either as a lump-sum credit against their income tax, or (for those without income) as a cash benefit. Basic income closely resembles the tax-credit proposals put forward by Sir Edward Heath's Government in 1972.[6] As the only option currently available which is family-friendly, work-friendly and symmetrical between married and single, it is discussed in greater detail in Part 5 of this *Research Monograph.*

4. TAX-BENEFIT MODELS: MODEL FAMILY ANALYSIS

The ways in which Britain's tax and benefit systems undermine work incentives have been criticised for many years. Income tax,

---

4 See Glossary, below, p.143.

5 Treasury, *The Reform of Personal Taxation*, Green Paper, Cmnd. 9756, London: HMSO, March 1986.

6 Treasury and DHSS, *Proposals for a Tax-Credit System*, Green Paper, Cmnd. 5116, London: HMSO, 1972.

national insurance contribution and local authority (council) tax – all increasing faster than prices and earnings – are charged on earnings below the entitlement levels for income support and a host of other means-tested benefits, to produce a structure which narrows differences in living standards between incomes in and out of work (*unemployment or income support trap*), between workers at different levels of gross earnings (*poverty trap*), and between small savers and those who spend to the hilt (*savings trap*). After publication of the first edition of *Moral Hazard*, I received letters from pensioners complaining that their life-time savings served only to disqualify them from means-tested benefits. Some were worse off than if they had not saved at all. They still are.

To analyse the processes at work, new jargon has emerged and new analytical techniques have been devised, relying heavily on computer models. Since 1975 the Department of Health and Social Security (DHSS) and the Department of Social Security (DSS) have produced a series of Tables comparing *spending power* out of work and at different levels of earnings for different hypothetical or model families. Spending power in work is defined as gross earnings *less* income tax, NI contribution, local authority tax, rent and (sometimes) work expenses, *plus* child benefit and any means-tested benefits to which there may be entitlement. Spending power out of work is defined as NI benefit and/or income support *plus* all means-tested benefits to which there is entitlement *less* rent and local authority tax. For measuring work incentives, spending power is a more useful concept than net income, which only takes into account income tax, NI contribution and child benefit. The DHSS and DSS Tax Benefit Model Tables for the years 1979-94 provide the statistical basis for much of the analysis in this *Monograph*.

When using the Model Tables great care is necessary, because some of the spending power figures rest on assumptions that limit their validity. In real life, variations in housing costs, housing tenure and work expenses can tilt the balance for or against a particular job offer, while in the Model Tables all the families are assumed to live in subsidised local authority rented housing, pay 'average' local authority rents and rates (or council tax), and take up all the means-tested benefits to which they are entitled. So the Tables project an over-optimistic image of the real world. 'Average' travel-to-work expenses were included in some of the early Tables, but childcare costs have never been shown, and in this *Monograph* neither is included unless specified.

For these reasons, all that model family analysis can do – and it does it well – is to show whether those parts of the tax and benefit systems that can be quantified (tax liabilities, child benefit, local authority rents and means-tested benefits) produce large enough margins between spending power in and out of work (or from differ-

FIGURE 1.2:
The 'Why Work?' Syndrome, April 1994
Married man with two children aged 4 and 6

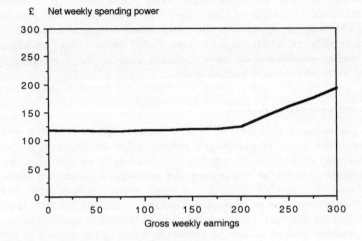

Source: DSS Tax Benefit Model Tables, April 1994.
Assumptions: Work expenses of £10 per week; average local authority rent and council tax.

rent levels of gross earnings) to preserve work incentives. Over time the Tables also show whether incentives for families in the assumed circumstances have increased or diminished. What they cannot show and will never be able to show is the number of people affected by moral hazard, nor the effects of the tax/benefit structure on the supply and distribution of labour, nor the costs and distributional effects of different reform options.

Figure 1.2, based on the April 1994 DSS Tax Benefit Model Tables, shows the situation of a single-wage couple with two small children living in local authority housing, with weekly work expenses of £10. Average male manual earnings in April 1994 were £281 a week. Earnings of £125 were required to match nil earnings on income support. At earnings of £200 the gain from full-time work (by comparison with income support) was still only £6. At earnings of £300 the gain was £77.

5. TAX-BENEFIT MODELS: ACTUAL FAMILY ANALYSIS

During the 1980s, partly to fill the gaps in model family analysis, a new generation of (micro-simulation) models was developed, based on analysis of the incomes of families participating in the Family Expenditure Survey. The new models do not replace the old ones but serve different purposes: in particular, they are used to estimate the costs and distributional effects of different tax and benefit reform options. One such model written by Holly Sutherland, who is director of the Microsimulation Unit, Department of Applied Economics, University of Cambridge, has been used in Part Five of this *Monograph*, to estimate the distributional effects of a system of convertible tax credits/basic incomes. Called *Polimod*, the Cambridge model resembles the tax-benefit models used by the Treasury and the Institute for Fiscal Studies (IFS).

6. REPLACEMENT RATIOS

A *replacement ratio* is the income received when out of a job, expressed as a proportion of income from employment (either previous, present or prospective). For unemployed claimants the earnings that matter are prospective earnings. Replacement ratios related to previous earnings, though easier to calculate, are unhelpful, because an unemployed person would not normally have been in his previous job unless it had been financially worthwhile.

Replacement ratios can be defined in terms of net income or net spending power. So long as the figures fed into the calculations refer only to net income (earnings *less* income tax and NI contribution *plus* child benefit), the replacement ratios can be generalised for the working population as a whole. Such comparisons are, however, unhelpful, for it is the excluded variables (like housing costs, local tax, travel-to-work and childcare costs) which often tilt the balance for or against acceptance of a given job offer. Net spending power replacement ratios, on the other hand, do take into account housing costs, but cannot be generalised for the population as a whole.

7. HOUSING COSTS

Between April 1979 and April 1994, average local authority rents increased by a factor of six and housing association rents grew even faster, with further increases in the pipeline. Government Ministers seem oblivious to the effects of their housing policies on work incentives. In 1979 comparatively few lower-paid families owned their own homes, but escalating rents and the mortgage boom of the 1980s greatly increased owner-occupation. The disincentive effects of the mortgage trap are disproportionately large, partly because of the sums involved and partly because there is no equivalent of housing benefit for mortgagors who take lower-paid jobs. In August 1993 the balance of interest on mortgages above £150,000 was excluded from income support. In April 1994 the limit was reduced to £125,000 and from April 1995 it was reduced to £100,000. The labour market effects of these changes remain to be seen.

8. PERIOD UNDER REVIEW

Most of the statistics in this study cover the period April 1979 to March 1995. Looking ahead, the November 1994 Budget contained no major change of direction. From October 1995 unemployed people with mortgages will get no help from the state during the first six months of unemployment (existing mortgage holders) or nine months (new mortgage holders), after which interest on the first £100,000 of a mortgage will be paid in full. So for mortgagors who are still unemployed after six or nine months and whose homes have not been repossessed, the disincentive to take work in the formal economy will be greater than before, unless the job is sure to last. The married couple's income tax allowance remains frozen at £1,720 (the last uprating was in April 1990) and is now also restricted to 15 per cent. In April 1995, the part-time trap described in Part Two, Section 6 of this study (below, p.45) was reduced but not removed by a £10 supplement with family credit for parents of families working 30 hours or more a week. And the DSS now operates three definitions of full-time work: 16 hours, 24 hours and 30 hours.

PART TWO

How the Traps Are Baited: 1994 Compared with 1979 and 1982

---

1. SEVEN TRAPS

By the end of the 1970s, for a small but growing section of the community, pay differentials had become largely meaningless, it was no longer worthwhile to accumulate small savings, and it was becoming increasingly difficult to find jobs that paid more than the dole. Since 1979, despite many benefit cuts and some of the biggest income tax reductions in history, the same problems remain. At the top of the earnings distribution, tax liability has fallen dramatically, but at the bottom – and some way above it for families with children – out of each £1 earned, wage earners are still charged income tax, national insurance (NI) contribution and local authority tax at the same time as their benefit entitlements are being withdrawn; and low-income pensioners can still find their life-time savings swallowed up in reduced benefit entitlement and extra tax. Seven 'traps' stand out:

- The unemployment/income support trap

- The invalidity trap

- The poverty trap

- The lone-parent trap

- The part-time trap

- The lack-of-skills trap

- The savings trap

None of these problems is unique to Britain. Throughout much of Western Europe the relative gains from working have fallen, but in Britain the situation is particularly bad. Unlike our main competitors, for instance, we have no benchmarks by which to ensure that out-of-work benefits stay above the minimum amounts necessary for good health and social participation whilst retaining a sufficient gap between incomes in and out of work. In North America and much of mainland Europe, budget standards[1] derived from studies of human need and consumer preferences are used as reference points for wages, taxes and benefits, but in Britain we rely on hunches, guesses and political priorities.

2. THE UNEMPLOYMENT/INCOME SUPPORT TRAP

The unemployment trap is the oldest and most damaging of the traps. First identified in the late 1960s, it acquired its present name in the early 1980s, as a result of persistent questioning by Sir Ralph Howell MP:[2] it refers to a situation in which people are encouraged to stay out of work for longer than is strictly necessary or to move to the underground economy, because a return to work in the formal economy would either reduce their spending power or bring a net gain too small to make the effort financially worthwhile. For the purposes of this study a net gain of £25 for a full week's work, after allowing for work expenses, is taken to be the minimum necessary in 1994-95 to offset the disadvantages of work. Some people may be satisfied with less, most expect more.

Changes since 1979

Since 1979, most benefits have either been cut or are being allowed to 'wither on the vine' by upratings in line with prices instead of earnings.[3] Table 2.1 summarises the relevant changes.[4] Earnings-related supplements were abolished in 1982, sickness benefit was replaced by statutory sick pay in 1983, the child additions payable with unemployment and sickness benefit were phased out by 1984, all the main out-of-work benefits except invalidity benefit have been made reckonable for tax, and in 1988, following Sir Norman Fowler's Social Security Review,[5] there was major restructuring of

---

[1]   See Part 5, 'Criteria', below, p.94, and Glossary, p.144.

[2]   Ralph Howell, *Why Work? A Challenge to the Chancellor*, Conservative Political Centre, 1976; *Why Work? A radical solution*, Conservative Political Centre, 1981.

[3]   Because earnings increase faster than prices on average, indexation to prices means that benefits represent an ever-decreasing proportion of earnings.

[4]   In *Turning the Screw: Benefits for the Unemployed*, A.B. Atkinson and John Micklewright identified 17 changes in NI unemployment benefit and 15 changes in supplementary benefit/income support between 1979 and 1988. (A.B. Atkinson, *Poverty and Social Security*, Hemel Hempstead: Harvester Wheatsheaf, 1989, Ch.8.)

[5]   Secretary of State for Social Services, *Reform of Social Security*, Cmnd.9517, London: HMSO, June 1985.

Table 2.1:
Main Social Security Benefit Changes, 1980-95

1980:	Pension upratings linked to prices instead of earnings.
1982:	Earnings-related supplements with NI unemployment and sickness benefit abolished. All NI benefits except invalidity benefit start to become reckonable for income tax; likewise supplementary benefit.
1983:	NI sickness benefit replaced for most claimants by statutory sick pay.
1984:	Child additions with NI unemployment and sickness benefit abolished. Child additions with long-term NI benefits for widows and invalidity pensioners uprated by less than inflation.
1988:	Major restructuring of means-tested benefits. Income support (IS) replaces supplementary benefit (SB), Social Fund replaces SB single payments; rate rebates reduced from 100% to 80% for people on IS; water and sewerage rates no longer payable with income support. Big cuts in housing benefit for the lower paid, not for the unemployed. Family credit replaces family income supplement and is payable for six months at a time instead of twelve. Family credit, housing benefit and rate rebates all become means-tested instead of income-tested. Free school meals and free welfare milk restricted to families in receipt of IS.
1991:	Child benefit uprated, but concentrated on first child in each family. Child Support Act tightens up liability to maintain regulations.
1993:	Child Support Agency established. Community charge replaced by council tax. Families on IS get 100% rebates of their council tax (as with local authority rates).
1994:	Childcare disregard of £40 introduced with family credit.
1995:	NI invalidity benefit (tax-free) replaced by NI incapacity benefit (taxable). Major restructuring of mortgage interest with income support.

means-tested benefits. In 1991 the structure of child benefit was also altered. Instead of the same flat-rate amount for every child, the first child in each family now gets more than the others, even though large families are more at risk of poverty and work disincentives than small families.

Making benefits reckonable for income tax was a key change which immediately widened the gap between incomes in and out of work. Its purpose was not to tax people with no income other than their social security benefits, but to ensure that claimants do not pay less tax than working people on the same income. Under Britain's cumulative PAYE system a tax-free benefit qualifies its recipient for refunds of income tax paid earlier in the same tax year, or for tax-free earnings at the end of the tax year.

Under the new system income tax refunds are still payable (again due to the cumulative nature of PAYE) but they are much smaller than before. Invalidity benefit and child benefit are the only major social security benefits still tax-free. For the minority of invalidity pensioners with other income this exemption operates like a double tax relief, first on their state benefits and then on their other income, but it is scheduled to go when invalidity benefit is replaced by incapacity benefit in 1995. Some people say that child benefit too should be taxed, but the arguments for doing so appear weaker, for when tax-free child benefit was introduced (in 1979) it replaced child tax allowances as well as taxable family allowances. Now that husbands and wives are taxed independently, there is also the difficult question of which parent should be taxed.

One result of the changes listed in Table 2.1 is that nearly 68 per cent of out-of-work claimants were on income support in August 1993, compared with 64 per cent in November 1983 and 48 per cent in November 1979.[6] Only one in five unemployed people receives NI unemployment benefit (Figure 2.1). At the edges of the labour market there is little incentive to pay NI contribution, and after Job Seekers Allowance is introduced (in 1996) there will be even less. Regular workers are being penalised for the 'sins' of a minority, as a result of which more are joining the irregulars.

Paradoxically, given Lady Thatcher's and John Major's dislike of welfare dependency, they have between them presided over a bigger increase in it than any of their predecessors. For the main effect of the policies of the last 15 years has been to reduce out-of-work living standards and work incentives simultaneously – and to replace the unemployment trap by the income support trap, which is more damaging because it reduces the incentive to save as well as to work and may well also jeopardise family solidarity.

Between 1979 and 1994 average manual earnings rose about three times, while retail prices rose 2½ times, so the gap between incomes in and out of work might have been expected to widen. In some cases it has, but not by enough to remedy the problem. Figure 2.2 shows spending power in and out of work for the same two-child family as before, in 1982 and 1994. In each case the figures start at approximately one-third and finish just above average male manual earnings. If anything the 1994 situation looks worse.

---

6   *Sources*: 1979 and 1983: *Annual Abstract of Statistics*, 1985 Edition, Table 3.16.

1993: *Hansard*, 14 January 1994, col.299.

FIGURE 2.1:
Eligibility for Unemployment Benefit, August 1993

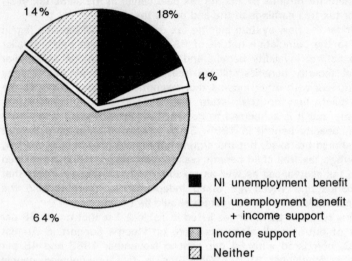

- ■ NI unemployment benefit
- □ NI unemployment benefit + income support
- ▨ Income support
- ▨ Neither

Source: Hansard, 14 January 1994, col. 299.

FIGURE 2.2:
The Unemployment Trap, April 1982 and 1994
Married Couple + 2 children aged 4 and 6

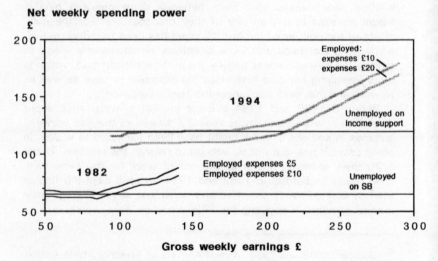

Source: DHSS and DSS Tax Benefit Model Tables, April 1982 and 1994, plus author's own calculations.

Replacement ratios

Table 2.2 compares supplementary benefit (SB) in 1982 with income support (IS) in 1994, for the same two-child family. Because of the complexity of the regulations and the many changes that have taken place, the figures are not strictly comparable, but they are close enough to show trends. Although income support has kept up with inflation, the extras have been severely cut, so one would expect a big improvement in *replacement ratios*.[7] Instead, at below average male manual earnings, replacement ratios for families with children have remained obdurately high and in some cases have gone up. For example, at three-quarters average male manual earnings the family in Table 2.2 had a spending power replacement ratio of 93 per cent in 1994, compared with 85 per cent in 1982 during year one of unemployment (SB ordinary rate) and 98 per cent during year two (SB long-term rate).

Table 2.3 includes more family types. Again the figures take three-quarters average manual earnings as the reference point, but the supplementary benefit figures are slightly higher than in Table 2.2, being based on 120 per cent of the SB scale rates. Certainly the gap between incomes in and out of work has widened for 16-17-year-olds (who are no longer entitled to benefit) and for 18-24-year-old householders (whose benefit has been cut), but for families with children and families where women are the breadwinners (or would be if the system made it worthwhile) replacement ratios remain high, even assuming work expenses of only £10 a week. In real life, the incentives of individual claimants hang precariously on their housing costs and work expenses. For mortgagors, the escape points from the unemployment trap are much higher than those shown here. Certainly there has been no break-through and if wage inflation had been contained the figures would have been worse.

Gross weekly earnings necessary to be £25 a week better off in paid work than unemployed

Small amounts of undisclosed earnings are considered 'fair game' by the unemployed. One result of cutting out-of-work benefits when unemployment is high is to increase the number of unemployed claimants who work 'on the side'. When they run into debt, they have little choice. Some years ago, according to research on a run-down council estate near Exeter, £25 'on the side' was considered

[continued on p.34]

---

7   See Glossary, below, p.137.

TABLE 2.2:
Spending Power Replacement Ratios:
Couple with two children aged 4 and 6, April 1982 and 1994

A. APRIL 1982

Income	£		£	Outgoings	£
		SB long-			
SB ordinary rate	43·05	term rate	52·65		
Child benefit	10·50		10·50	Rent	14·60
				Rates (inc.	
Heating addition	1·65		1·65	water)	6·40
Free school meals	2·25		2·25		
Free welfare milk	1·40		1·40		
Rent rebate	14·60		14·60		
Rate rebate	6·40		6·40		
TOTAL	79·85		89·45	TOTAL	21·00
Spending power*	58·85		68·45		

Replacement ratio at 75% average male manual earnings (work expenses £5)

	85·0%	98·0%

* Plus single payments, additional requirements in each case.

TABLE 2.2 (continued)

B. APRIL 1994

Income	£	Outgoings	£
Income support	94·60	Rent	36·42
Child benefit	18·45	Council tax	11·00
		Water rates	
Free school meals	4·04	(estimated)	3·40
Free welfare milk	2·76		
Housing benefit	36·42		
Council tax benefit	11·00		
TOTAL	167·27	TOTAL	50·82
Spending power	116·45	(+ Social Fund loans)	

Replacement ratio at 75% average male manual earnings (work expenses £10)

	93·0%

TABLE 2.3:
Replacement Ratios, April 1982 and 1994
Net spending power on supplementary benefit/income support as a
proportion of net spending power at 75% average manual earnings,
DHSS/DSS model families

Family type	1982 Work expenses £5	1994 Work expenses £10
	%	%
MALE BREADWINNERS		
Single non-householder aged 16-17	26	
Single non-householder aged 18 +	34	
Single householder - any age	59	
Single aged 16-17		00
Single aged 18-24 non-householder		24
Single aged 18-24 householder		32
Single aged 25 + non-householder		30
Single aged 25 + householder		40
Married couple	81	60
Married couple + 2 children aged 4 and 6	92	93
Married couple + 4 children aged 3,8,11,16	108	95
FEMALE BREADWINNERS		
Single non-householder aged 16-17	42	
Single non-householder aged 18 +	55	
Single householder - any age	90	
Single aged 16-17		00
Single aged 18-24 non-householder		35
Single aged 18-24 householder		56
Single aged 25 + non-householder		44
Single aged 25 + householder		70
Married couple	109	93
Married couple + 2 children aged 4 and 6	99	100
Married couple + 4 children aged 3,8,11,16	108	104

Source: DHSS Tax Benefit Model Tables, April 1982; DSS Tax Benefit Model
Tables, April 1994; author's calculations.
Assumptions: Working families: as in DHSS Model Tables, except for work
expenses, which are as shown.
Out-of-work families: spending power on SB assumed to be 120% of scale
rates, on IS assumed to be IS allowances and premiums plus free school
meals and free welfare milk.
Gross weekly earnings: Men £100 in April 1982, £212 in April 1994;
women £60 in April 1982, £137 in April 1994.

FIGURE 2.3:
Percentages of average manual earnings required
to be £25 a week better off than on the dole, April 1994

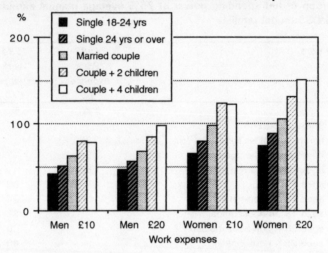

Source: DSS Tax Benefit Model Tables, April 1993, and author's calculations.

Note: Average male manual earnings £281 a week; average female manual earnings £182 a week.

acceptable.[8] That is why a minimum gain from full-time paid work of £25 is used as a bench-mark in Figure 2.3, which shows the percentages of average male and female manual earnings necessary in April 1994 to be £25 a week better off in full-time work, assuming work expenses of £10 and £20 a week. Women are particularly at risk because on average they earn less.

EXAMPLE: In April 1994, to be £25 a week better off than on the dole, an 18-24-year-old woman paying average local authority rent and council tax, but with work expenses of £20, needed to earn £136 a week (compared with average female manual earnings of £182).

8   Bill Jordan, Simon James, Helen Kay and Marcus Redley, *Trapped in Poverty? Labour-Market Decisions in Low-Income Households*, London: Routledge, 1992. See also: H. Dean and P. Taylor-Gooby, *Dependency Culture*, Brighton: Harvester Wheatsheaf, 1992; and E. Evason and R. Woods, 'Poverty, Deregulation of the Labour Market and Benefit Fraud', *Social Policy & Administration*, Vol.29, No.1, 1995.

EXAMPLE: In April 1994, to be £25 a week better off than on the dole, a married man with two children aged 4 and 6, with rent of £36·42, council tax of £11 and work expenses of £20 a week, needed to earn £240 (compared with average male manual earnings of £281).

3. THE INVALIDITY TRAP

Although the invalidity trap is different from the unemployment trap, both correlate with situations where earnings potential net of tax is low in relation to out-of-work benefits. For many invalidity pensioners the problem is aggravated by high living costs, low (often variable) earnings potential and the rigidity of the benefit regulations. Invalidity benefit (IVB) is higher than NI unemployment benefit and (as already noted) tax-free.

The official statistics, which show 1·5 million invalidity pensioners in 1992/93 compared with 600,000 in 1978/79,[9] prompt the question whether the nation is really so unhealthy? Are so many people really unable to work? Are they 'scroungers'? Or do the benefit regulations trap people with minor disabilities and mental disabilities into inactivity? Whatever the answers, it is important to get the figures into perspective. Invalidity benefit was not introduced until 1971, so an increasing case-load is inevitable, as surviving claimants grow older. Also, although the overall case-load continues to rise, the figures for successful new claims have gone down (Figure 2.4 and Appendix 3, below, p.130). New claims statistics show cyclical fluctuations, indicating that people with disabilities find it more difficult to get jobs when unemployment is high than when it is low.

Disability working allowance, introduced in April 1992, was intended to mitigate the invalidity trap, but it only goes to a few thousand people, and being heavily means-tested it replaces the invalidity trap with the poverty trap.[10] It is unlikely that incapacity benefit will solve these problems, although it will remove the anomaly of double tax relief.

---

[9] *Hansard*, 3 December 1993, cols. 813-16, and 18 May 1994, cols. 523-24.

[10] Between April 1992 and 1993, disability working allowance was awarded to fewer than 3,000 people (*Social Security Statistics, 1993*). See also Social Security Advisory Committee, *In work – out of work: The role of incentives in the benefits system*, The Review of Social Security Paper 1, SSAC, July 1994, pp.29-30.

FIGURE 2.4:
Invalidity Benefit Statistics, 1971-94

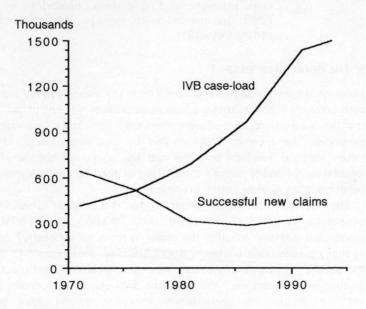

Sources: Case-Load: *Social Security Statistics*, 1989, and Social Security
Departmental Report, 1994.
New Claims: *Hansard*, Written Answer, 1 February 1994, col.
690.
Note: The case-load figures refer to a particular month in each year,
whereas the successful new claims are spread out over 12 months
and may include two or more spells commencing for the same
person.

4. THE POVERTY TRAP

Contrary to public perceptions, the poverty trap is not the result of
kindly governments boosting the incomes of the lower paid.
Although low pay plays a part, so does tax. Single people and
families with earnings below income support levels are charged
income tax, NI contribution and council tax at the same time as their
means-tested benefits are being withdrawn. During the last 12 years
the poverty trap has changed, but not this basic fact.

At the bottom of the earnings distribution, marginal gains from
each extra £1 earned are at best 25 pence, sometimes only 2 pence

and occasionally negative. The main difference is that today's poverty trap is more heavily concentrated at the bottom of the earnings distribution, due partly to benefit restructuring and partly to average wage increases above the rate of inflation. At the bottom of the earnings distribution, spending power has barely kept up with prices. In Table 2.4 it is assumed that the families earned one-third, two-thirds and average male manual earnings in both years. By 1994 those on average male manual earnings were £28 a week better off in real terms than in 1982, compared with weekly gains of £4 at two-thirds average male manual earnings and £1 at one-third.

TABLE 2.4:
Who Gained What?
Spending power at one-third, two-thirds and average male manual earnings, single-wage couple with two children aged 4 and 6, April 1982 and 1994, £s per week

Year	Gross weekly earnings (rounded)	Spending power: current prices	Spending power: April 1994 prices	Real gain 1982-1994
	£	£	£	£
1982	45·0	70·0	125·0	
	90·0	71·0	126·0	
	134·0	86·0	153·0	
1994	94·0	126·0	126·0	1·0
	187·0	130·0	130·0	4·0
	281·0	181·0	181·0	28·0

Sources: DHSS/DSS Tax Benefit Model Tables; author's calculations.
Note: To make the figures comparable, £3·40 has been deducted from DSS spending power figures in 1994, for water rates.

The mechanism of today's poverty trap is summarised in Table 2.5. Although the escape points are lower in relation to average earnings than in 1982 (Table 2.6), the effects (Figures 2.4 and 2.5) are broadly similar. Fewer families face marginal tax rates above 100 per cent, but miniscule gains of two or three pence out of each extra £1 earned (as happens to families in receipt of housing benefit, council tax benefit and family credit) do comparable damage.

[continued on p.39]

TABLE 2.5:
How the Poverty Trap Worked in 1994-95

	Deduction rates from each extra £ of gross earnings %
1. *Income Tax (excluding higher rate tax):*	
Income below £66·25 (single), £99·33 (single-wage married couple or lone parent)	0·00
Income between £66·25 - £123·94 (single), £99·33 - £157·02 (single-wage married couples or lone parents)	20·00
Income above £123·94 (single), £157·02 (single-wage married couple or lone parents)	25·00
2. *National insurance contribution (Class 1):*	
Earnings below £57	0·00
Earnings between £57 and £429:	
on first £57	2·00
On balance	10·00

	Benefit deduction rates from each extra £ of net income %
3. *Housing benefit:*	
Income equal to or less than the *applicable amount*	0·00
Income above the *applicable amount*	65·00
4. *Council tax benefit:*	
Income equal to or less than the *applicable amount*	0·00
Income above the *applicable amount*	20·00
5. *Family credit:*	
Income equal to or less than the *applicable amount*	0·00
Income above the *applicable amount*	70·00

Note: Major changes to benefit regulations were introduced in April 1988. Incomes for family credit, housing benefit and council tax rebate are assessed on net incomes *after* deductions for income tax and national insurance contribution. Free school meals and free welfare milk are restricted to families in receipt of income support. For each means-tested benefit, there is an *applicable amount* which varies according to family size, age of children and other circumstances. In-work benefits are withdrawn using the tapers shown in the Table. Housing benefit is reduced by 65% of net income above the applicable amount, council tax benefit by 20% and family credit by 70% of net income. In 1994-95, these tapers, when superimposed on income tax and national insurance contribution (Class 1, not contracted-out rate), produced marginal tax + benefit deduction rates for a couple with two children aged 4 and 6, paying average local authority rents and council tax, as shown below:

Married couple + 2 children Gross weekly earnings (£)	Marginal tax + benefit deduction rates (%)
<55	nil
55	85
56	101
57-73	86-87
74	90
75-171	95-97
172	93
173	134
174-207	80-81
208	117
209-429	35
430 to higher rate tax threshold	25

TABLE 2.6:
Poverty trap escape points
In percentages of average manual earnings, April 1982 and 1994

	MALE		FEMALE	
	1982	1994	1982	1994
	%	%	%	%
Single householder	72	41	120	63
Single + 2 children aged 4 and 6	96	74	161	115
Married couple	85	54	143	83
Couple + 2 children aged 4 and 6	99	74	165	115
Couple + 4 children aged 3,8,11,16	106	107	178	165

As a result of the 1988 benefit changes, the poverty trap for single people and couples without children has become shorter but sharper. Figure 2.5 shows the marginal gain or loss (in pence) from each extra £1 earned. As before, the curves for each year start at approximately one-third average male manual earnings and finish just above the average. In 1982 rent and rate rebates were with-

FIGURE 2.5:
The Poverty Trap, April 1982 and 1994
Single-wage married couples

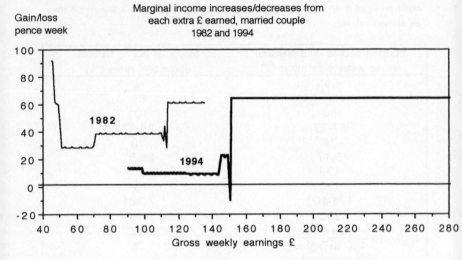

Marginal income increases/decreases from
each extra £ earned, married couple
1982 and 1994

Source: DHSS Tax Benefit Model Tables, April 1982; DSS
                 Tax/Benefit Model Tables, April 1994.

Assumptions: Single-wage couples living in local authority rented
                 accommodation, paying average rent and rates/council tax,
                 no allowance for work expenses. Other assumptions as in
                 the DHSS/DSS Tables.

drawn by 23 or 33 pence out of each extra £1 earned, whilst the
tapers today are 65 per cent of each extra £1 of net income with
rent rebates (now called housing benefit) and 20 per cent with
council tax benefit. In theory, housing and council tax benefits are
adjusted every time earnings change, itself a huge disincentive and
administrative hassle.

Children and the poverty trap

Families with children are disproportionately at risk of the poverty
trap. With family income supplement (FIS) some families stood to
lose over 100 per cent of each extra pound earned, although in
practice this was usually avoided by making FIS awards payable for
a year at a time, the idea being that the FIS ceilings would have
been raised before a family's award came up for renewal.
Nevertheless, there was nothing in law to prevent people from being
worse off by earning more. The irony is that family credit (FC) does
so little better. It is inconsistent to claim that 97 per cent marginal

FIGURE 2.6:
The Poverty Trap, April 1982 and 1994
Single-wage couple with two children aged 4 and 6

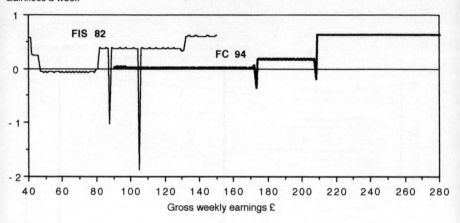

Marginal income increases/decreases from
each extra £ earned, couple + 2 children
April 1982 and 1994

Source: DHSS Tax Benefit Model Tables, April 1982; DSS Tax
                   Benefit Model Tables, April 1994.
Assumptions: Single-wage couples with two children aged 4 and 6
                   years, living in local authority rented accommodation,
                   paying average rent and rates/council tax, no allowance
                   for work expenses. Other assumptions as in the
                   DHSS/DSS Tables.

tax rates damage incentives at the top of the earnings distribution
but do not do so at the bottom. High marginal deduction rates also
encourage abuse. While FIS was payable for 12 months, family
credit is payable for only six. Either way, it is difficult for the DSS to
prevent families from increasing their family credit entitlements by
reducing their earnings during the weeks before they put in a claim.

Looking at Figure 2.6, the flat contours riven by crevasses are
remarkably similar in both years. The deeper crevasses of FIS came
about at points in the income scale where free welfare milk and free
school meals were withdrawn. The 1988 reforms overcame this
problem by removing entitlement to free welfare milk and free
school meals, but created new, smaller crevasses at points on the
earnings scale where housing benefit and family credit are
withdrawn. In 1982, for the family portrayed here, the escape point

FIGURE 2.7:
The Poverty Plateau
Working age households, April 1994

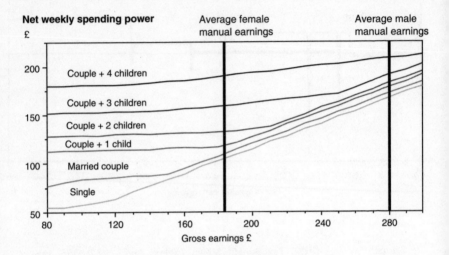

Source: DSS Tax Benefit Model Tables, April 1994.

from the poverty trap was £132 (just below average manual earnings). By 1994, it was £209 a week (just below three-quarters average male manual earnings). It looks like an improvement, but it is due more to the earnings explosion of the 1980s than the legislation.

The poverty plateau

At grass-roots level the disappearance of differences in spending power over a wide range of earnings is not seriously disputed, but is played down by government. Within that range people find themselves on a plateau where extra effort and extra skills go unrewarded. The size of the plateau depends on family composition and housing costs: the bigger the family, the older the children, the higher the rent, the broader the plateau (Figure 2.7).

EXAMPLE: Because of the poverty trap, in April 1994 a couple with four children aged 3, 8, 11 and 16 were only £36 a week better off earning £300 a week than

£55 a week, without taking into account their costs of working. Yet £300 was above average male manual earnings at that time.

5. THE LONE-PARENT TRAP

Lone mothers and their children are among the most vulnerable members of society. Most of the mothers have low earnings potential and most – if they are in paid work – have childcare costs to pay. Since 1982 their situation has changed dramatically. In April 1982, for families represented in the DHSS Tax Benefit Model Tables but assuming work expenses including childcare of £20 a week, net weekly spending power at average female manual earnings was £52, compared with roughly £47 during year one on supplementary benefit (SB) and £55 thereafter. Income support is much tougher. Gone are the SB long-term additions, 'single payments' and 'additional requirements'. Instead there is a schedule of allowances and premia that have been pared to the bone. Rent and council tax are still payable, but claimants now have to pay their water and sewerage rates in full. Passport benefits like free school meals and free welfare milk remain and, for exceptional cases, there is a system of interest-free loans through the Social Fund, which are afterwards deducted from the borrower's weekly benefit cheque.

If the nub of the lone-parent trap in 1982 had been over-generous benefits, by now it would surely have melted away. Instead, the number of lone parents on income support continues to rise.[11] Problems remain which the DSS on its own cannot rectify. Childcare is one of them. In France, after two years in receipt of lone-parent benefit, or when the youngest child reaches three years of age, lone parents are expected to take paid work, which is feasible because every French child is guaranteed a nursery school place from the age of three. In Britain, taxpayers' money is spent on allowing lone parents to choose whether or not to take a job until their youngest child is 16. Mothers who want to work face a lethal mixture of low wages, high tax and high work expenses. Alternatives, such as targeting scarce resources on high-quality nursery education for the children and job-training for the mothers, seem not to have been considered.

---

[11] In May 1992, 957,000 lone-parent families were on income support.

FIGURE 2.8:
The Lone-Parent Trap, 1994
Net spending power, lone mother with two children
aged 4 and 6, before and after childcare disregard

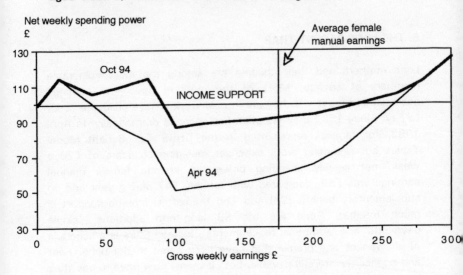

Sources: *Hansard,* 6 July 1994, cols. 227-32 and 20 July 1994,
                cols. 255-56; plus author's calculations.

Assumptions: (1) Childcare costs: nil on IS earning £15; £25 working 16
                hours (earning £40); £40 working 24 hours earning £60 or
                £80; £70 working full-time earning £100 - £300.
                (2) Travel costs: nil earning £15 or £40, otherwise £10 a
                week.
                (3) Rent £36.42, council tax £8.30.

Enabling lone mothers to go out to work instead of subsidising
them to stay on the dole is the only sure way to alleviate their
problems. In October 1994 the Government broke new ground by
introducing a childcare disregard with family credit, but it is of
limited value because the maximum amount is £40 a week
regardless of the number of children needing childcare. In a 1991
survey the Policy Studies Institute found that average expenditure
on childcare by working lone parents was £24·60 a week,[12] and the

---

[12] *Sources*: (1) A. Marsh, and S. McKay, *Families, Work and Benefits*,
London: Policy Studies Institute, 1993. (2) A. Marsh, and S. McKay,
'Families, Work and the Use of Childcare', *Department of Employment
Gazette*, August 1993.

DSS used this to justify their £40 disregard. They seem not to understand that an expenditure survey in this context is misleading, because families cannot spend money they do not have. In January 1994 a summary of responses from over 3,000 members of the National Childminding Association produced average weekly charges of £60 per child. Indeed, in London the median weekly charge for full-time childcare was £70 per child.[13]

Figure 2.8 shows the lone-parent trap before and after introduction of the disregard, for a mother with two children aged 4 and 6. Childcare and travel costs are assumed to vary according to the hours worked. For mothers whose costs are higher than those assumed here, the escape points from the trap are higher – and vice versa. Although clearly better than nothing, the disregard is so low that unless childcare costs are below £40 and travel costs are zero, a mother's best bet is to work part-time so that she can maximise her family credit, reduce her childcare costs and see more of her children. The disregard is therefore likely to produce 'clustering' of earnings at levels where this occurs and to introduce a new part-time trap.

6. THE PART-TIME TRAP

This recent innovation is caused by reducing the hours' threshold for eligibility to family credit. With family income supplement, two-parent families had to work 30 hours and lone parents had to work 24 hours in order to qualify. With family credit the threshold was originally 24 hours for all families with children, but in April 1992 it was reduced to 16 hours. Given the high marginal deduction rates associated with family credit, a change of this sort was bound to produce a part-time trap.

EXAMPLE: In 1994-95, assuming earnings of £3.75 an hour, it made only £5 a week difference in terms of spending power whether a married man (or woman) with two children worked 16 hours a week for £60 or 40 hours a week for £150 (Figure 2.9).

---

[13] *Pay and Conditions: A Negotiating Guide for Childminders*, Bromley, Kent: National Childminding Association, 1994.

FIGURE 2.9:
The Part-Time Trap, 1994
Couple with two children, hourly earnings £3.75

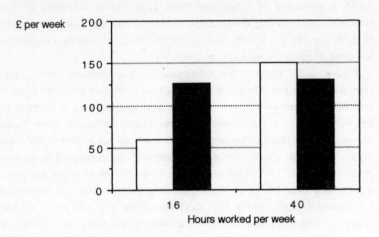

□ Gross weekly earnings ■ Net weekly spending power

Source: DSS Tax Benefit Model Tables.

7. THE LACK-OF-SKILLS TRAP[14]

Throughout the developed world long-term unemployment correlates increasingly with lack of marketable skills. In Britain there is mounting concern about skill training and large sums of public money are invested in it, yet we persist with tax and benefit systems which work in the opposite direction. For example, instead of benefits being conditional on study or training, the opposite is the case. To qualify for Training for Work, participants must have been continuously unemployed for at least 26 weeks, and for some programmes the qualifying period is 52 weeks.

In 1942 Beveridge recommended that for 'boys and girls there should ideally be no unconditional benefit at all; their enforced abstention from work should be made an occasion of further

---

[14] This section relies heavily on Part 6 of Discussion Paper No. 1, *Basic Income and the Labour Market*, ed. Hermione Parker, Basic Income Research Group, 1991. See also Ewart Keep and Ken Mayhew, 'Education, Workforce Training and Economic Performance in Britain', in C. Buechtemann and D. Soloff (eds.), *Human Capital Investments and Economic Performance*, London: Sage, 1994.

training'.[15] Unfortunately, he made no specific proposals. During the 1960s a system of mandatory, income-tested grants was developed for first-degree students, which opened the doors to higher education for millions of low-income families. Those grants are now being replaced by student loans. There are economic arguments in favour of loans, because a large part of the gains from higher education is captured by the student in terms of increased lifetime earnings.[16] But a disadvantage is that fewer children from low-income families may become students.

Illogical support 'system' for the 16-17 age group

When children reach 16 years of age their benefit status depends on whether or not they remain in full-time education and whether it is academically or vocationally oriented. Sixteen-year-olds staying on at school remain the financial responsibility of their parents who continue to receive child benefit for them, while school-leavers count as separate benefit units. Until 1988 school-leavers could claim supplementary benefit in their own right, and some did so whilst waiting to go to university or other higher education or skill training. Since 1988 they have not normally been entitled to anything except a course of youth training.

So the question arises who is (or should be) financially responsible for 16-17-year-olds when they are neither training nor in a job. If the parents, should not child benefit continue to be paid? If the young people themselves, should they not have guaranteed access to training and/or study until they are 18, plus some form of guaranteed income? At present many have little hope of finding regular employment, being at best semi-literate and semi-numerate and coming from homes where nobody is in paid work.

In 1991/92 an estimated 7 per cent of boys and 6 per cent of girls left school with no grades at all.[17] The question arises why British children are allowed to leave school at fixed chronological ages, regardless of individual achievement. In Germany, in order to move up a grade or leave school, pupils have to satisfy their teachers that they are ready to do so. Although it made sense to withdraw income support from 16-17-year-olds, it is wrong to leave

---

[15] Sir W. Beveridge, *Social Insurance and Allied Services*, Cmd.6404, London: HMSO, 1942, paras. 122, 131 and 349 (quotation cited from para.131).

[16] E.G. West, *Britain's Student Loan System in World Perspective: A Critique*, IEA Current Controversies No.9, London: Institute of Economic Affairs, June 1994.

[17] *Social Trends 1995*, Table 3.15.

income maintenance for this vulnerable age group in a vacuum. The German dual system, combining academic and vocational education and supported by income-tested grants and loans, would be more appropriate.

Fragmented and conflicting provisions

For reasons lost in the mists of time, students and trainees of all ages are uniquely excluded from income support – Britain's safety net of last resort – on the grounds that they are unavailable for work. Instead they are stranded in a no-man's-land between the Department of Employment, the Department of Education and Science, and the Department of Social Security. Parliamentary Questions get nowhere, because no Department wants to take responsibility. Most people think that the DSS, through income support, provides an income guarantee below which no Briton is allowed to fall. But this is not so. In certain, narrowly defined circumstances the DSS allows unemployed claimants to draw income support whilst attending part-time courses of not more than 21 (soon to be 16) hours a week, 'but only if they are continuing to make a sustained effort each week to find a job and are prepared to leave the course immediately a suitable vacancy becomes available'.[18] Consequently, people whose low attainments make them virtually unemployable are prevented from bettering themselves.

Because income support is more readily available than training allowances, and because income tax, NI contribution and council tax cut in at such absurdly low wages, small businesses have difficulty paying trainee wages that can compete with the dole, while employees (or potential employees) are deterred from investing in their own training. In August 1989 Sir John Cassels, a former Director General of NEDO,[19] blamed Britain's skill shortage on a 'low productivity/low wage syndrome... reinforced by low investment in human resources'.[20] He put forward proposals reminiscent of the German system, but omitted income maintenance.

In the Autumn of 1989 the Confederation of British Industry (CBI) published proposals for a skills revolution, with similar targets but including Exchequer-funded training credits for 16-year-olds, and replacement of local authority education maintenance allowances by a national, discretionary maintenance allowance

---

18 *Hansard*, 14 June 1994, col. 361.

19 National Economic Development Office.

20 J. Cassels, *Britain's Real Skill Shortage*, London: Policy Studies Institute, 1990.

'for those denied educational opportunity through poverty and for those who are genuinely unable to find an employer training place through disadvantage, disability or in areas of high unemployment'.[21]

Youth credits have been introduced, but they go to the employers. Apart from the Labour Party's Commission on Social Justice,[22] no more has been heard of educational maintenance allowances. A huge carrot is necessary to rectify this situation.

8. THE SAVINGS TRAP

One advantage of national insurance benefits is the encouragement they can give to voluntary savings. Few people save voluntarily if they think it will reduce their future benefit entitlement when out of work or retired, and those who have saved are incensed to discover they have been 'conned'. In the pensioner lobby the savings trap raises more hackles than any other. While huge inducements in the form of income tax reliefs are given to taxpayers who can afford to save large sums, elderly people who have scrimped and saved for a modest but comfortable old age discover that their thrift leaves them no better off – and sometimes worse off – than their spendthrift neighbours.

It is well known that means-tested welfare puts voluntary saving at risk and the greater the reliance upon means tests the greater the scale of the problem. In 1942 Beveridge warned that:

'Provision by compulsory insurance of a flat rate of benefit up to subsistence level leaves untouched the freedom and the responsibility of the individual citizen in making supplementary provision for himself above that level... But to give the fullest possible encouragement to voluntary insurance and saving, it is important to reduce to a minimum the cases in which assistance has to be given subject to consideration of means.'[23]

Retirement pensioners and invalidity pensioners are particularly at risk, but they are by no means alone. Unknown to most people, unemployment benefit (and the new jobseeker's allowance) is reduced or eliminated if the claimant has an occupational or personal pension. Since 1980, Beveridge's warnings have been increasingly disregarded. Instead of raising the basic pension (and invalidity bene-

---

[21] Confederation of British Industry, *Towards a Skills Revolution*, CBI, 1989.

[22] *Social Justice: Strategies for National Renewal*, The Report of the Commission on Social Justice, London: Vintage, 1994, p.134.

[23] Sir W. Beveridge (1942), *op. cit.*, Appendix F, para. 16 (3) (my emphasis). See also W. Beveridge, *Voluntary Action*, London: George Allen & Unwin, 1948.

FIGURE 2.10:
The Savings Trap: Occupational Pensioners, April 1994

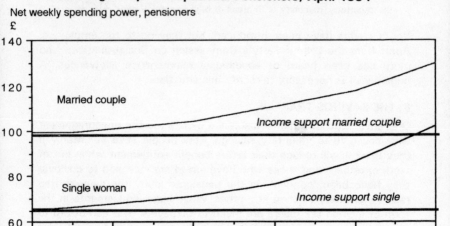

Net weekly spending power, pensioners

Source: Age Concern.

Assumptions: Single woman aged 75, rent £35 a week, council tax £5.
Couple, husband aged 65, rent £50 a week (including service charge), council tax £7.

fit) in line with earnings – maintaining its value at a modern minimum throughout a lengthening old age (or disability) and withdrawing it from better-off claimants through a more progressive income tax – pensions have been indexed to prices (so that they wither away) and the tax system has been made less progressive. When Ministers imply that price indexation protects living standards they are misleading the public. For short periods it may be true, but not in the long term. Had the state basic pension been uprated since 1948 in line with prices only, by 1994 it would have been only £22·45 a week, instead of £57·60.[24]

The pensioner poverty trap

The effects of the current situation are complicated and varied. Figure 2.10 illustrates the situation in April 1994 for occupational pensioners, for a single woman aged 75 or over, and a couple where the husband is 65, on the assumption that each receives the full basic state pension, no income from savings or investments, but an occupational pension of between zero and £100 a week. Very few

---

[24] *DSS Abstract of Statistics*, 1994, Table 5.1 (a).

single women have occupational pensions of £100 a week. In 1992, 47 per cent of single women pensioners aged 75 or over had occupational pensions, but half of them received less than £24·30 a week. Of pensioner couples aged under 75, an estimated 73 per cent had occupational pensions, but half of them received less than £54·80 a week.[25]

For occupational pensioners in rented housing, every additional £1 of income above the claimant's applicable amount results in a loss of 65 pence in housing benefit and 20 pence in council tax benefit. Home-owners face a maximum taper of 20 pence because they are not entitled to housing benefit. But if they are mortgagors, the savings trap is accentuated, because their mortgage interest is paid in full so long as they are receiving income support, but not at all if they are not. Pensioners on income support may also be able to receive other help, such as age-related and disability premiums, lump-sum payments from the Social Fund and maximum (as opposed to partial) help with certain National Health Service charges.

EXAMPLE: A 75-year-old single pensioner paying rent of £35 a week and council tax of £5 a week needs an occupational pension of about £90 a week in order to be £25 a week better off than on income support. A 65-year-old married pensioner paying rent of £50 a week and council tax of £7, also needs an occupational pension of about £90 a week.

For pensioners with savings or investment income the system also imposes wealth tests. Income support is not payable to a single person or a couple with over £8,000 capital. Housing benefit and council tax benefit are not payable if savings (or capital) are over £16,000. Savings over £3,000 are assessed as £1 of extra weekly income for every £250 (or part of £250) over £3,000. So every £250 of savings or investment income over £3,000 results in a 65 pence reduction in housing benefit and a 20 pence reduction in council tax benefit. Thus, pensioners with £5,000 savings are treated as though they had an extra £8 a week income.

---

[25] *Hansard*, Written Answer, 24 January 1995, cols. 129-30. See also *The Pensions Debate: A Report on Income and Pensions in Retirement*, London: Age Concern England, 1994, pp.20-21.

PART THREE

Scale of the Problem and Priority for Change

Once incentives to work and to save are undermined and family networks weaken, expenditure on social security becomes uncontrollable and the extra tax needed to pay for it exacerbates the problem.

However, although it is relatively easy to show that Britain's tax and benefit systems weaken self-reliance and that the situation is getting worse, not better, it is not possible to estimate the numbers of families and individuals affected. Even if it were possible to estimate the number of people who are better off not working than working, it would be incorrect to assume that the same number 'choose' not to work. In practice, many people work for very little financial gain, some because they do not realise how small the gain is, some because they value the long-term advantages of remaining in the labour force, and others because they like to work. Others are so offended at the insinuation that their labour is worth less than the dole – or needs to be supplemented by means-tested benefits – that they prolong their job search, hoping a more lucrative job offer will come their way. But it may take months and the unemployment statistics reflect every delay.

1. GOVERNMENT THE MAIN CULPRIT

Instead of blaming itself for what is happening, Government under-estimates the scale and complexity of the problem and blames its victims. A man who delays going back to work until he finds a job that pays more than the dole is not so much 'scrounging' as playing by the rules of a government-imposed system. Of course there are people who are out to milk the system: the more complex the regulations the easier it becomes. But in Britain the steady growth in claimant numbers since 1979 – despite repeated benefit cuts – suggests that more than 'scrounging' is involved.

Those affected are not just the unemployed. Anyone with low earnings potential is at risk. Moreover, low earnings in this context means low in relation to out-of-work benefit entitlements. In Britain today an unskilled family man in poor health has almost no chance of becoming financially independent. The more children he has and the higher his rent, the smaller his chances are. By 1985 an estimated 40 per cent of families with four or more children were out of work (sick or unemployed), and those who were in work were in the upper end of the earnings distribution. Six years later, in 1991, 45 per cent of families with four or more children were out of work.[1] By now the figure may be approaching the 50 per cent mark.

By disaggregating the problem it can be shown that low earnings defined in this way correlate with family responsibilities, disability and lack of skills. Most at risk are the following:

- The unskilled or semi-skilled;

- People with disabilities, and those who care for them;

- Single-earner, two-parent families with children;

- Lone parents;

- Young adults;

- 'Third-agers' in their fifties and early sixties.

In its 1994 Departmental Report, in an attempt to show that the scale of the problem is declining, the DSS again turned survey evidence on its head. Instead of asking unemployed people what wages they require to gain (say) £25 a week by working, the DSS statisticians analysed Family Expenditure Survey (FES) data, discovered that fewer respondents with jobs had net incomes below 130 per cent of what they would get on the dole in the 1993 FES than in the 1985 FES, and rejoiced that DSS policies were succeeding. Unfortunately, all that the figures really show is a decline in the number of people who are prepared to work for practically nothing.[2]

2. BRITAIN'S CLAIMANT EXPLOSION

Table 3.1 shows changes in claimant numbers since 1978/79. Apart from an increase in the number of old-age pensioners (because of longer life expectancy), it is the work-tested, means-tested benefit programmes that have grown the fastest. The number claiming child benefit, much maligned as wasteful, is virtually unchanged. Yet it is families with children and young adults which are the main cause of escalating income support case-loads, reflecting their vulnerability to the poverty and unemployment traps.

This vulnerability is well known. It is the reason why children's allowances payable *in time of earning and not earning alike* were a

---

[1] *Hansard*, Written Answers, 21 January 1988, cols. 838-40, and 11 July 1994, cols. 395-98.

[2] DSS, *The Government's Expenditure Plans 1994-97*, London: HMSO, March 1994, Figure 16.

key assumption of the Beveridge Plan; that no British government has heeded Beveridge's advice is a key element in today's claimant explosion. While it is to the credit of Lady Thatcher's Government that the existence of moral hazard was officially recognised and the need to tackle it given high priority, it is to the discredit of successive administrations that the diagnosis has been simplistic and the policies adopted have made matters worse. Figure 3.1 shows that increasing supplementary benefit/income support caseloads are a product of the 1980s. From 1966 until 1976, supplementary benefit case-loads were remarkably stable, by the late 1970s they were starting to edge up, but it was not until 1981 that they took off.

TABLE 3.1:
Claimant Numbers, '000s

Benefit	1978/79	1982/83	1992/93	1994/95
NI basic retirement pension	8,602	9,232	10,055	10,056
NI unemployment benefit	492	975	654	625
NI invalidity benefit	610	737	1,439	1,705
aged 65 and over	38	55	219	n.a.
age 60-64	173	217	330	n.a.
age under 60	399	465	890	n.a.
Sup ben/income support	2,933	4,266	6,087	5,605
aged 65 and over	1,610	1,662	1,368	n.a.
age 60-64	202	249	263	n.a.
age under 60	1,121	2,355	3,456	n.a.
Child benefit	7,178	7,045	6,857	7,048
One-parent benefit	311	508	855	950
Family income supplement/Family credit	85	65	442	448
Rent rebate	2,667	3,580	3,105	3,186
Rent allowance	741	851	1,210	1,432
Rate rebate/ community charge benefit/council tax benefit	5,460	6,850	6,655	5,365

Sources: 1978/79 to 1992/93: *Hansard*, 3 December 1993, cols. 813-16, and letter from the DSS.
1994/95: *Hansard*, 18 May 1994, cols. 523-4.

FIGURE 3.1:
Supplementary Benefit and Income Support:
Working age claimants, 1966-93

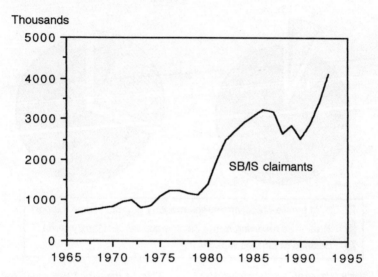

Thousands

Source: Social Security Statistics.

Today, approximately four times more working-age claimants receive income support than received supplementary benefit in 1978-79. Five times more families with someone in work receive family credit than received family income supplement. And over one million more households receive housing benefit. More families are at risk of disincentives and more children (including 40 per cent of under-fives) are being reared in families where evading or disobeying the law is necessary to keep out of debt. By August 1993 the total number of claimants, adult dependants and children receiving income support, was almost 10 million (over one in six of the population). Though outside the terms of reference of this study, the links between crime, especially juvenile crime, and the tax and benefit systems require close investigation.

3. FAMILIES AT RISK

It may be argued that examples relating to families at two-thirds or three-quarters of average male manual earnings are unrealistically low. Yet in 1991-92, when male manual earnings averaged £260 a week, an estimated 1 million working families with children had gross weekly incomes excluding state benefits below £180 and a further 1 million had between £180 and £260. All were working for 30 hours a week or more. Additionally, 1 million two-parent families

FIGURE 3.2:
Families on Income Support/Family Credit

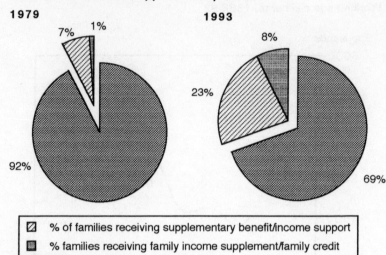

Source: Hansard, 16 December 1993, col. 836; 11 January 1994, cols. 24-26; 28 April 1994, col. 283.

and nearly 1 million one-parent families were out of work. So in 1991, before the peak of the last recession, roughly 2 million working families and 2 million out-of-work families – that is, over half of all families with children – were at risk of disincentives.[3] By 1993, 3½ million children (almost one in four of tomorrow's wealth creators) were being reared in families receiving income support, compared with under 1 million (7 per cent) in 1979 (Figure 3.2). Additionally (though not shown here), by 1993 nearly one-third of children in the under-five age group were being reared in families receiving income support and a further 7½ per cent in families receiving family credit.

For increasing numbers of children, social inclusion depends on both parents being in paid work. In 1991, out of 1·2 million families with below-average male manual earnings, nearly 1 million depended on a single wage, of whom over 80 per cent were two-parent families.[4] All such families are disproportionately at risk from the phasing out of the married couple's income tax allowance and the additional personal allowance for lone parents.

---

[3] Hansard, Written Answer, 11 July 1994, cols. 395-98.

[4] Ibid.

FIGURE 3.3:
Supplementary Benefit/Income Support, 1978-93
Claimants aged 16-17 and 18-24 years

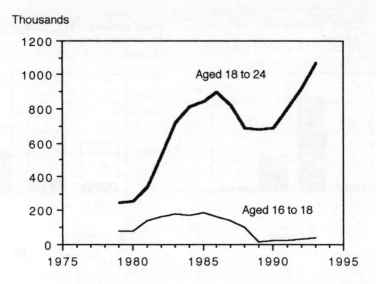

Source: Hansard, Written Answer, 26 January 1994, col. 267.

Young adults are a further cause for concern. Between 1978 and 1993 the number of 18- to 24-year-olds receiving income support rose from 252,000 to over 1 million. A similar growth in the number of 16- to 17-year-olds on benefit was prevented by removing benefit entitlement (Figure 3.3).

Much of the increase in benefit dependency is due to breakdown of the traditional family. By 1991, out of nearly 7 million families with children, 1·3 million were headed by lone mothers. Never-married (or single) mothers are more likely than other lone mothers to be on income support. In May 1992, out of 933,000 lone mothers receiving income support, almost a half had never been married.[5]

---

5   Department of Social Security, *Social Security Statistics 1993*, London: HMSO, Table A2.15.

FIGURE 3.4:
Lone Mothers by Age and Marital Status

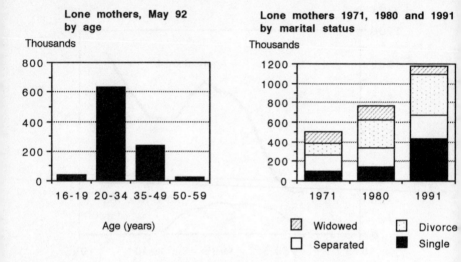

Lone mothers, May 92 by age

Lone mothers 1971, 1980 and 1991 by marital status

Sources: Social Security Statistics 1993, Table A2.15; *Hansard*, 2 December 1993, cols. 719-20.

4. NUMBERS CAUGHT IN THE POVERTY TRAP

In 1979, if one includes recipients of rent and rate rebates as well as family income supplement, an estimated 470,000 working families were affected by the poverty trap (Table 3.2). By 1993 the comparable figure was 675,000, with virtually no families affected by marginal deduction rates of over 100 per cent, but five times as many affected by rates of over 75 per cent. Further increases are expected – indeed, the poverty and unemployment traps are so closely linked that any sizeable decrease in one is likely to re-appear as an increase in the other. By the end of 1994 family credit was being paid to about 600,000 families.

TABLE 3.2:
Scale of the Poverty Trap:
GB, 1979 and 1993

Marginal deduction rates	Numbers affected			
	1979		1993	
	Families	Adults	Families	Adults
100% or more	30,000	50,000	nil	nil
75% but less than 100%	60,000	100,000	500,000	770,000
50% but less than 75%	180,000	290,000	90,000	125,000
40% but less than 50%	200,000	370,000	85,000	95,000
TOTAL	470,000	810,000	675,000	990,000

Sources: 1979: Letter to Sir Brandon Rhys Williams MP from the DHSS,
            29 June 1982.
            1993: Hansard, 24 February 1994, col. 367.

5. TOTAL NUMBERS AT RISK, 1979 AND 1989

Trying to estimate the number of families, adults and individuals
(including children) at risk of the various traps is like trying to
estimate the 'natural' or 'minimum' sustainable rate of
unemployment from old data. It is not feasible, for every increase in
the number of out-of-work claimants reduces still further the margin
of incentive between incomes in and out of work, further extends
the period of job search necessary to find a financially acceptable
job, and pushes up the 'natural' rate of unemployment a further
notch. Writing in 1982, I indicated the scale of the problem, by
using DHSS statistics showing the numbers of adults under
pensionable age who were: (a) dependent on supplementary benefit
(SB); (b) with incomes below SB levels (which they were not
receiving);[6] and (c) with incomes not more than 40 per cent above
SB levels. All are likely to be 'discouraged' in one way or another.
Figure 3.5 updates the 1979 DHSS figures to 1989, and includes
pensioners. The detailed figures are in Appendix 2 (below, p.129);
there can be no doubting the direction of change:

*Between 1979 and 1989 the number of pensioners at risk of
disincentives fell by 10 per cent, while the number of working-age
adults approximately doubled. Since 1989 the situation has
worsened. By 1994 some 4 million working-age adults were on
income support, compared with 1.4 million in 1979 and 2.9 million
in 1989.*

---

6   Either because they had not claimed their SB entitlements, or because
     they had no entitlement.

FIGURE 3.5:

Numbers at Risk, 1979 and 1989

Numbers of adults receiving supplementary benefit (SB) or with relative net resources below 140% SB in 1979; compared with numbers receiving income support (IS) or with relative net resources below 140% IS in 1989.

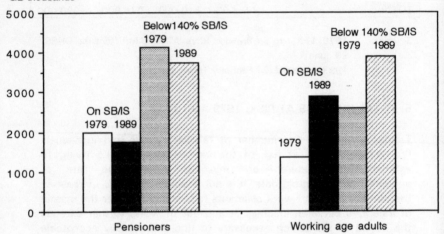

GB thousands

Source: Appendix 2, adapted from Steven Webb and Christopher Giles, *Poverty Statistics: A Guide for the Perplexed,* IFS Commentary No. 34, Institute for Fiscal Studies, January 1993, Tables 2,3 and 5.

6. EXPENDITURE OUT OF CONTROL

Unsurprisingly, given the number of people at risk of moral hazard, public expenditure on social security is out of control, especially expenditure on income support for people of working age and on housing benefit. Table 3.3 compares expenditure on the main social security benefits in 1979-80, 1988-89 and 1994-95, all at 1994-95 prices.

TABLE 3.3:
Social Security Expenditure: 1994 prices, £ million

Benefit	1979-80 outturn	1988-89 outturn	1994-95 plans
NI retirement pension (basic)	22,312	25,577	26,444
Ditto earnings-related	3	515	1,805
NI unemployment benefit	1,653	1,501	1,716
NI sickness benefit	1,658	260	387
Statutory sick pay	-	1,218	25
NI invalidity benefit	2,511	4,104	6,374
Ditto earnings-related	8	452	1,391
Income support/supp. benefit (pensioner)	1,698	2,515	3,985
Income support/supp. benefit (working age)	2,541	7,769	12,507
Child benefit	7,054	6,124	6,106
One-parent benefit	109	243	318
Family credit/family income supplement	68	534	1,276
Rate rebate	1,126	2,367	-
Council tax benefit	-	-	1,630
Rent rebates/ allowances, housing benefit	2,007	5,118	9,979

Sources: *Growth of Social Security*, DSS, 1993, Table 9a; Social Security Departmental Report, DSS, 1994, Table 1.

The figures highlight the changing rôle of the Department of Social Security. Instead of poverty prevention, as envisaged by Beveridge, it is more concerned with unsustainable programmes of poverty relief. Between 1979 and 1994 the fastest growing programmes were not pensions or child benefit, nor even invalidity benefit, but family credit (up 20-fold at constant prices); income support for working-age families (up five-fold) and housing benefit (also up five-fold). The latest move (announced in the November 1994 Budget) is to cap housing benefit, but since local authorities have a responsibility to house homeless families, the effect will probably be to shift the burden from the DSS onto the local authorities initially, followed by increases in council tax – and council tax benefit – instead.

7. POLARISATION OF THE LABOUR MARKET

Finally, is there a correlation between the tax and benefit systems and the labour market opportunities of semi-skilled and unskilled

FIGURE 3.6:
Unemployment Rates by Sex and Socio-Economic Group
1979 compared with 1990

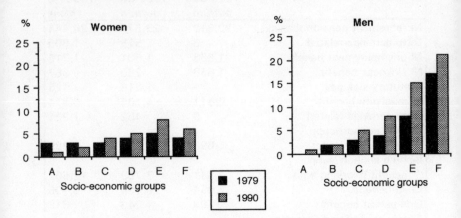

Key: A = Professional B = Managers C = Intermediate
D = Skilled E = Semi-skilled F = Unskilled

Source: General Household Survey 1992, Table 7.5.

men and women? Although the return of long-term unemployment is by no means entirely due to the tax and benefit systems, the relatively low unemployment rates of women at the bottom of the earnings distribution do suggest correlations. So long as the father's earnings are above the entitlement levels for family credit, the mother's earnings are unaffected by the traps, but if the father is made redundant, relatively few mothers have the earning capacity to take over as breadwinner without running headlong into the poverty trap. Fathers with young families and non-earning wives are also disproportionately at risk of moral hazard, especially if they are unskilled or semi-skilled.

Figure 3.6 compares unemployment rates by socio-economic group in 1979 and 1990, for both women and men. In both years unemployment averaged 4 per cent for each sex, yet the incidence of unemployment between the different socio-economic groups could hardly be more different. In 1979, unemployment rates for women were roughly the same across all the socio-economic groups. By 1990 the differences were more marked, with semi-skilled manual women and personal service workers eight times more likely to be unemployed than professional women. But it is the figures for men that are startling. Even in 1979, semi-skilled and

FIGURE 3.7:
Distribution of Work in Two-Adult Households, 1975-93

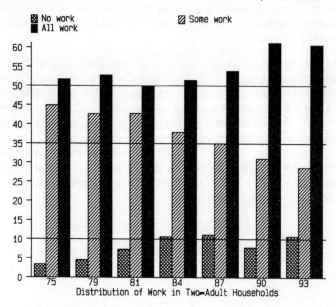

Source: Paul Gregg, Jonathan Wadsworth, *More Work in Fewer Households?*, NIESR Discussion Paper No. 72, 1994, Figure 4.

unskilled male manual workers were eight times more likely to be unemployed than male professionals. By 1990, the year before unemployment took off, a semi-skilled male manual worker was 15 times more likely to be unemployed than a professional man and an unskilled manual worker was 21 times more likely to be out of work.

Although no correlation between the incidence of unemployment and the tax and benefit systems has been demonstrated statistically, the likelihood is supported by studies showing polarisation in the labour market between two-earner and no-earner families. Writing for the National Institute of Economic and Social Research (NIESR) in 1994, Paul Gregg and Jonathan Wadsworth showed how the distribution of work in two-adult households has changed (Figure 3.7), and drew the following conclusions:

'UK employment has moved cyclically in the 1980s and 1990s, but benefit dependency has grown secularly... Even with constant employment rates over time, changes in the distribution of employment in favour of multiple earner households implies that a rising number of other households will have no work and hence can explain rising benefit dependency. The number of workless households rose sharply in the recession of the early 1980s but nearly all the subsequent recovery in employment occurred in households where one person was already in work, leaving on balance many more multi-income households and more workless households. Britain is now characterised by work-rich and work-poor families.'[7]

In the November 1994 edition of the *Employment Gazette*, Frances Sly reported a disproportionate growth in labour market participation rates by mothers between 1984 and 1994.[8] An estimated 64 per cent of mothers with children under 16 are now in paid work, compared with 55 per cent in 1984, but the greatest increase has been among women with children aged under five (up from 37 per cent in 1984 to 52 per cent in Winter 1993/94). Among mothers with employed husbands/partners, 68 per cent are in employment, but where the husbands are unemployed, only 24 per cent of mothers are working.

7   Paul Gregg and Jonathan Wadsworth, *More Work in Fewer Households?*, Discussion Paper No. 72, London: National Institute of Economic and Social Research, 1994 (Conclusions and Policy Implications).

8   Frances Sly, 'Mothers in the labour market', *Employment Gazette*, November 1994.

PART FOUR

Causes of the Problem

1. INCOHERENT POLICY-MAKING

As a result of benefit changes since 1979, Britain is becoming a residual welfare state. Work disincentives, it is alleged, result from over-generous benefits so the remedy is to cut benefits.

In reality, work incentives are affected by a range of factors, including taxation as well as benefits. Moreover, different benefits have different effects. If a league table were composed with incentive-friendly benefits at the top and incentive-hostile benefits at the bottom, child benefit would come top, NI benefits would come second and means-tested benefits would come bottom. Income support would come rock-bottom. Child benefit and NI widowed mother's allowance sharpen work incentives because recipients can build on them through paid work. Income support blunts incentives, because coming off it – unless the new job is well paid and sure to last – is too risky.

Some components of today's 'traps' can be traced to design faults in the Beveridge Plan; some to the way it was implemented; some to changes in tax incidence at the expense of the lower paid; some to the failures of family policy; and all to incoherent policy-making within and between different government departments. Whenever a universal benefit is replaced by means-tested provision (dental care, eye care, school milk, school meals, or the short-lived minimum grant for students), whenever rents, council tax, interest rates or fares to work increase faster than net earnings, incentives at the margin are damaged. Certainly the 1988 social security reforms rationalised the benefit system, but the DSS is only one of many players. Policy changes that cut in-work living standards tighten the knot of disincentives regardless of which Department makes them. The difference is that it is the DSS which is left to pick up the pieces. First come Ministerial assurances that those in need will be protected, then come Treasury protests that DSS expenditure is out of control. It has happened time and again and will continue until the whole paraphernalia of income redistribution (taxes as well as benefits) is comprehensively reformed.

Since 1979, first the DHSS and now the DSS have been used as agencies for the relief of poverty induced by other government departments. More and more families are being driven into dependence on means-tested benefits and then vilified for it. Meanwhile, increasing numbers of the 'nearly poor' (small savers and hard workers) find themselves too 'rich' to qualify for means-tested benefits but too 'poor' to gain worthwhile amounts from lower rates of income tax.

Widely publicised arguments in the media that universal benefits are too expensive disregard the long-term effects of means-tested welfare on wealth creation, voluntary saving and family life, and take for granted that means-tested, work-tested welfare can be administered on a massive scale without running out of control. Yet the system is already out of control.

How did it happen?

Why has government so signally failed? Five factors, taken together, show how it came about; one underlying reason explains why. The *how* factors, with which the bulk of this chapter is concerned, can be summarised as follows:

- A benefit system that pays people for not working, not studying and not training, subsidises low wages, and rewards family break up.

- A tax system that pauperises the lower paid, by forcing them into dependence on means-tested benefits.

- Unprecedented and continuing cuts in housing subsidies.

- An inadequate and fragmented system of support for children and young adults; and a tax system that penalises single-earner couples.

- Complexity beyond belief which is getting worse, not better.

Why did it happen? The need for budget standards

Of the many reasons *why* it happened, perhaps the most insidious is the haphazard approach to other people's requirements that characterises large parts of British society and is reflected at Westminster, in Whitehall and by the media. In 1991 Mr Norman Lamont, then Chancellor of the Exchequer, stated that unemployment was a price worth paying,[1] but nobody at the Treasury counted the cost to families deprived of their livelihoods. They could not do so, because the budget standards methodology pioneered by Seebohm Rowntree in 1901,[2] and later used by

---

[1] 'Rising unemployment and the recession have been the price that we have had to pay to get inflation down. That price is well worth paying.' (*Hansard*, Oral Answers, 16 May 1991, col. 413.)

[2] In his study of poverty in York: B.S. Rowntree, *Poverty: A Study of Town Life*, London: Macmillan, 1901.

Beveridge to estimate the benefit levels necessary to avoid poverty, has been replaced by the simplistic assumption that 'real' poverty (unquantified and undefined) no longer exists.

Budget standards address the question: *How much does it cost to live?* Without an answer to that question government is targeting blindfold: some people get too much and others not enough. *'By necessaries'*, wrote Adam Smith in 1776, *'I understand not only the commodities which are indispensably necessary for the support of life, but whatever the custom of the country renders it indecent for creditable people even of the lowest order, to be without'*, adding, by way of illustration, that in Scotland leather shoes had become indispensable for men, though not for women or children.[3] Noticeable for its absence in Smith's definition is any distinction between absolute and relative poverty. Noticeable for its inclusion is the emphasis on social as well as physiological necessities (although Smith used the word 'necessaries').[4]

2. A BENEFIT SYSTEM THAT PAYS PEOPLE FOR NOT WORKING, NOT SAVING AND BEING 'POOR'

Between 1948 and 1982 most out-of-work benefits rose faster than prices, but so did earnings. It was a combination of other factors that narrowed the gap between them, for example, the introduction of earnings-related supplements with unemployment and sickness benefit in 1966, increasing taxation of the lower-paid resulting in increasing tax refunds when out-of-work, and the erosion of family income support for working families. In 1982 most NI earnings-related supplements were abolished. Since then almost all social security benefit rates have lagged behind earnings and the tax refund anomaly has been largely removed. So in theory the gap between incomes in and out of work should have widened and in a few areas it has, yet the benefit payrolls still grow like topsy, resulting in pressures for further benefit cuts and further tightening of the benefit regulations.

NI unemployment benefit

Beveridge-style national insurance benefits are different from the Bismarckian social insurance benefits used elsewhere in Europe. The former are flat-rate amounts with dependency additions (in theory enough to live on), while the latter are fixed proportions of previous earnings (whether or not you can live on them). So long as the 'Bismarck' proportions are not set too high and benefit is related to earnings net of tax (or is itself taxable), it is relatively easy to preserve the necessary gap between incomes in and out of work.

---

[3] Adam Smith, *The Wealth of Nations* (1778 edition), Book V, Ch.2, Article 4, 'Taxes upon Consumable Commodities', Everyman Edition, London: J.M. Dent, 1947, pp.351-52 (my emphasis).

[4] See Part 5, Section 2: 'Criteria' (below, pp.94-96) for further discussion of budget standards.

The disadvantages of Beveridge-style flat-rate benefits are, *first*, that the more effective protection provided at the bottom of the earnings scale is at the expense of the majority of wage and salary earners, since it is impossible to pay flat-rate benefits in amounts that are worthwhile to the majority without damaging work incentives amongst the lower-paid; *second*, that Beveridge's dependency additions for wives and children represent larger percentages of previous earnings for family men than for single people. In April 1994, for example, NI unemployment benefit at £45·45 a week equalled 32 per cent of gross earnings for a single person on half average male manual earnings, but 52 per cent (including spouse addition of £28·05) for a married man. In theory this effect will go when Job Seeker's Allowance is introduced and the adult dependency addition is abolished. In practice, as happened when the child additions were removed in 1984, the main effect will be to increase dependence on income support.

Figure 4.1 shows that the unemployment trap did not widen between 1948 and 1994 on account of increases in flat-rate NI unemployment benefit, which fell in relation to earnings after 1965 and reached an all-time low during the 1980s. It was between 1967 and 1981, when earnings-related supplements were payable, that NI unemployment benefit contributed to the trap. Since 1981, those effects have gone, due to abolition of the earnings-related supplement and the child additions. The pernicious side-effect has been to increase dependence on income support.

Income support an 'unpredictable and damaging' minimum wage

For every unemployed person or lone mother, but not for people who are in paid work, income support grossed up for income tax, NI contribution, council tax, housing costs, and work expenses, acts as a *de facto* minimum wage, made all the more unpredictable and damaging because it varies with the number and ages of the claimant's dependants. In this sense income support is identical to supplementary benefit, while family credit (which was supposed to remedy the problem) is identical to family income supplement.

The lesson of the last 15 years is that governments which want people to work and to save, must first make it worthwhile for them to do so, no matter how many children they have, how low their earnings or how small their savings. National assistance,[5] wrote Beveridge,

'must be felt to be something less desirable than insurance benefit; otherwise the insured persons get nothing for their contributions'.[6]

---

[5] Introduced in 1948, national assistance was the equivalent of today's income support.

[6] Sir William Beveridge, 1942, *op. cit.*, para.369.

FIGURE 4.1:
NI unemployment benefit and income support as percentages of gross average male manual earnings, 1948-94

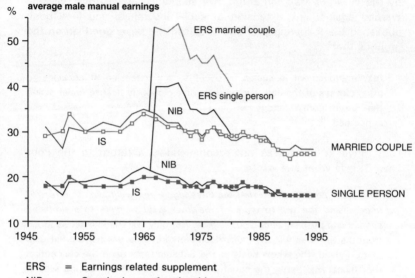

ERS = Earnings related supplement
NIB = Standard rate of national insurance unemployment benefit
IS = Income support, formerly supplementary benefit, formerly national assistance

Source: DHSS/DSS *Abstract of Statistics.*

And in another passage:

> '...to give the fullest possible encouragement to voluntary insurance and saving, it is important to reduce to a minimum the cases in which assistance has to be given subject to consideration of means'.[7]

Instead, income support is worth more than NI benefit, regular workers and small savers are treated worse than idlers and spendthrifts and the whole nation counts the cost.

Paying people not to work

An even more fundamental flaw in all forms of social insurance and social assistance can be summarised as follows:

> A country that pays people for not working and for being poor, ends up with more 'unemployed' people and more 'poor'.

---

[7]   Sir William Beveridge, 1942, *op. cit.*, App. F, para.16 (3).

Unknown to most people, this flaw was brought to the attention of Britain's war-time government in August 1942 (three months before publication of the Beveridge Report) in a pamphlet published by the *Western Mail and Echo*. In it economist Juliet Rhys Williams warned against any extension of social insurance, and in a book published the following year she criticised the Beveridge Plan on the grounds that

'any improvement in scales of benefits, any extension of pensions to other classes of the community, will come perilously near to undermining the profit-motive altogether where the wage-earning classes are concerned'.[8]

Lady Rhys Williams was not recommending a return to the Poor Law. This is what she wrote:

'There can be little doubt that the Beveridge Plan...will have the effect of undermining the will to work of the lower-paid workers to a probably serious and possibly dangerous degree. Not only will the idle get as much from the State as will the industrious workers, they will get a great deal more. Indeed, the whole basis of the Scheme rests upon the conception that those who serve the community by working and producing wealth must not on any account receive any State assistance or reward, but must be heavily taxed instead.'[9]

Lady Rhys Williams's solution was a novel one:

'*The prevention of want must be regarded as being the duty of the State to all its citizens, and not merely to a favoured few...* The new relationship would be expressed by the actual signature of a contract between the individual man or woman of eighteen and over, and the State, whereby the State would acknowledge the duty to maintain the individual and his children at all times, and to ensure for them all the necessities of a healthy life. The individual, in his turn, would acknowledge it to be his duty to devote his best efforts to the production of the wealth whereby alone the welfare of the community can be maintained.'[10]

---

[8] J. Rhys Williams, *Something To Look Forward To: A Suggestion for a New Social Contract*, Cardiff: Western Mail and Echo Limited, August 1942; and London: Macdonald & Co., 1943.

[9] J. Rhys Williams, *ibid.*, p.141, quoted in H. Parker, *Instead of the Dole*, London: Routledge, 1989, pp.121-22 (my emphasis).

[10] J. Rhys Williams, 1943, *ibid.*, pp.145 and 147 (emphasis in original).

The practical result of the contract was to be the weekly payment of £1·05 for each man, £0·95 for each woman (paid in her own right), and £0·50 for each child. All the rates were close to subsistence level. The scheme was designed to be revenue neutral assuming a social security tax on all other income at a flat rate of 45 per cent.[11] *The logic behind the proposal and what still makes it revolutionary, is that benefit becomes a base on which to build through paid work or savings, instead of a trap from which low earners cannot escape.*

Although Lady Rhys Williams's proposals were not taken up, her ideas were influential. In the United States they reappeared in amended form as negative income tax, and they fitted admirably with the proposals for *convertible tax credits*[12] of £6 a week for married couples, £4 for single people and £2 for every child, put forward by Sir Edward Heath's Government in 1972.[13] At the time of the 1979 General Election the Conservative Party was committed to tax credits. Had the party stood by its commitment, the UK might now have convertible tax credits, or *basic incomes*,[14] of about £40 for married couples, £26 for single people and £13 for each child. This option is investigated in Part 5.

Paying people for being poor

Just as out-of-work benefits can add to unemployment, so means-tested benefits can add to poverty. Of course, some degree of means-tested welfare will always be necessary. Without it taxation would have to be at levels that would themselves damage incentives. Yet the experiences of the past two decades raise questions about the scale of means-tested welfare that is economically appropriate and socially desirable. In 1982 the argument also concerned the way in which means-tested welfare had developed in Britain, in particular the proliferation of separate, uncoordinated benefits. The 1988 benefit reforms integrated income support with family credit, housing benefit and rate rebates, but this too raises problems. For instance, the single combined taper for housing benefit and council tax benefit makes it difficult to improve work incentives, especially while rents and council tax are increasing faster than prices.[15]

---

[11] In 1943 the standard rate of income tax was 50 per cent.

[12] See Glossary, below, p.143.

[13] Treasury and DHSS, *Proposals for a Tax-Credit System*, Green Paper, Cmnd.5116, London: HMSO, October 1972.

[14] See Glossary, below, p.143.

[15] Martin Evans, David Piachaud, Holly Sutherland, *Designed for the Poor – Poorer by Design? The Effects of the 1986 Social Security Act on Family*

FIGURE 4.2:
Percentages of Income Taken in Income Tax, NI Contribution and Local Authority Tax, April 1979 and April 1994

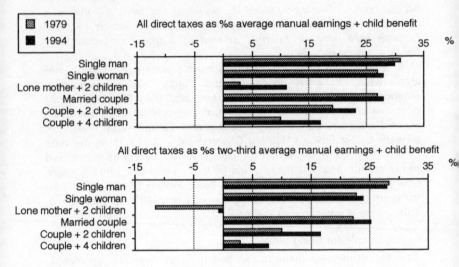

Source: Appendix 1, below, p.127.

Another problem is the fallacy that means-tested welfare can be administered on a mammoth scale (using computers) without fear of abuse. In reality the opposite is more likely to be true, for stigma vanishes when millions of people are on the 'social', as does respect for the law when the regulations are unenforceable.

3. TAX REGARDLESS OF ABILITY TO PAY (or 'TRAP')

The myth of falling taxes

A large part of the increase in social security expenditure since 1979 is tax-induced. Although income tax *rates* have fallen (especially the higher rates), income tax *allowances* (which are much more important to the lower-paid) have barely kept up with earnings, while NI contributions and local authority taxes have increased faster than earnings. Using figures for income tax, NI contribution and local authority rates/council tax published in the DHSS and DSS Tax Benefit Model Tables, April 1979 and April 1994, it can be shown that people with below-average earnings are paying more of

Incomes, Discussion Paper WSP/105, Welfare State Programme, Suntory-Toyota International Centre for Economic and Related Disciplines, London School of Economics, 1994, pp.87-92.

FIGURE 4.3:
Who Pays the Taxes?
Quintile groups of non-retired households, 1993:
Equivalised incomes

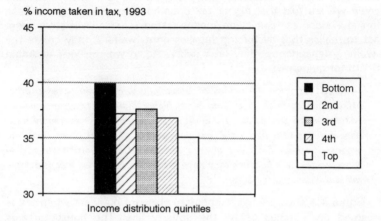

% income taken in tax, 1993

Income distribution quintiles

Source: Economic Trends, December 1994, Table D, p.40.

their incomes in tax today than in 1979. The lower their earnings and the higher the number of dependent children, the greater the tax increases (Figure 4.2).

EXAMPLE: A lone mother with two children aged 4 and 6, earning average female manual earnings, paid 11 per cent of her gross income (including child benefit) in tax in 1994-95, compared with 3 per cent in 1979.

EXAMPLE: A couple with four children aged 3, 8, 11 and 16, earning average male manual earnings, paid 17 per cent of their gross income (including child benefit) in tax in 1994-95, compared with 10 per cent in 1979.

So perverse have been the changes in tax incidence since 1979 that people in the bottom fifth of the income distribution now pay 40 per cent of their incomes (including state benefits) in tax compared with 35 per cent paid by the top fifth (Figure 4.3), a situation that would surely cause wage inflation if unemployment were not so high.

Tax-induced poverty

At the bottom of the earnings scale, the effects of tax regardless of ability to pay (or 'TRAP') resemble those of a giant snowball rolling downhill, getting bigger as it goes. At first the lower-paid try to recoup their tax losses through higher wages; then they are priced out of work; the underlying rate of unemployment goes up and the tax base is diminished; taxes go up again and the process is repeated, until the economy, like the snowball, falls apart. Time and again we are told that higher tax does not matter so long as those 'on low incomes' can claim means-tested rebates. Ministers seem not to realise that by forcing families onto 'welfare' they create the 'welfare dependency' they later decry. Again we can look to Adam Smith for guidance:

> *'A direct tax upon the wages of labour', he wrote, 'can have no other effect than to raise them somewhat higher than the tax... In order to enable him to pay a tax of one-fifth, his wages must necessarily soon rise, not one-fifth part only, but one-fourth... If direct taxes upon the wages of labour have not always occasioned a proportionable rise in those wages, it is because they have generally occasioned a considerable fall in the demand for labour.'[16]*

Figure 4.4 shows what happens to claimant numbers when tax is charged on incomes below the poverty line. The horizontal axis represents gross income and the vertical axis net income, and the 45° line tracks net incomes assuming no benefits and no income taxes. In Britain the original aim of social security was to fill the gap between the 45° line and the poverty line, the PAO triangle in the first diagram.

In the second diagram the line PA is the line of disposable income after adding in benefit, assuming a benefit withdrawal rate of 70 per cent. Tax does not come into it, because in a sane system poor people do not pay tax. Even so, by avoiding a 100 per cent benefit withdrawal rate there is benefit leakage to people with incomes above the poverty line (the shaded area above it).

The third diagram shows what happens when taxes are levied without regard to ability to pay: in this case council tax (chargeable at nil income), NI contribution and income tax (chargeable above the kink in the line BC). Incomes net of tax (the line BC) are dragged below the 45° line, the poverty gap is greatly enlarged and the number of people entitled to welfare benefits grows disproportionately (the shaded area OBAP), partly because the 70 per cent taper increases the amount of benefit leakage to people with pre-tax incomes above the poverty line, and partly because point A (where benefit ceases) is pushed into more thickly populated areas of the income distribution.

---

16 Adam Smith, *The Wealth of Nations* (1778 edn.),, Vol.2, Book V, Ch.2, Part 2, Article 3, 'Taxes upon the Wages of Labour', Everyman Edition, 1947, p.347 (my emphasis).

FIGURE 4.4:
Tax-Induced Poverty

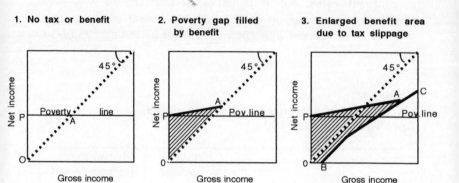

1. No tax or benefit

2. Poverty gap filled by benefit

3. Enlarged benefit area due to tax slippage

Ingredients of 'TRAP'

Excessive taxation of people on low incomes is the single most important reason why work incentives are still so small. 'TRAP' has three key ingredients:

- Income tax,
- NI contributions,
- Council tax.

(i) Income tax

At the bottom of the earnings distribution, income tax has fallen slightly for families without children, but has increased for families with children. How did that happen? The answer lies in the priority given to cuts in income tax rates. Top rates of income tax were reduced from 83 to 60 per cent in 1979, and to 40 per cent in 1988. Starting rates were reduced to 20 per cent in 1992. But tax allowances have barely kept up with earnings; married couple's allowance is being phased out; and child benefit (which replaced child tax allowances) has not even kept up with prices. In Table 4.1, child benefit is treated as a negative income tax. In both years, at

75

the levels of earnings shown, the child benefit entitlements of some families exceeded their income tax liability, hence the minus figures. Most gains are miniscule and most of the families with children pay more tax than before. Today it is government policy to reduce the standard rate of income tax to 20 per cent as soon as possible. This may attract votes, but in terms of work incentives it is poor targeting. A single person earning £10,000 a year stands to gain about £177, compared with £665 for a single person on £25,000 a year.

TABLE 4.1:
Percentages of earnings taken in income tax,
April 1979 and April 1994

	At average manual earnings		At two-thirds average manual earnings	
	1979	1994	1979	1994
	%	%	%	%
Single man	22	18	18	15
Single woman	17	15	10	9
Single woman + 2 children	-9	-3	-26	-17
Single-wage married couple	18	16	12	11
Single-wage couple + 2 children	9	9	-1	1
Single-wage couple + 4 children	1	3	-14	-8

Source: Appendix 1, below, p.127.

The perilous position of single-income families

Raising tax thresholds well above income support levels is a pre-condition for getting families with low earnings potential into work. It is not getting the priority it deserves. Big changes to income tax allowances were introduced along with independent taxation of husband and wife in 1990. Since then every taxpayer has been entitled to a *personal tax allowance* (£3,445 in 1995-96) below which no income tax is payable; married couples can also claim a *married couple's allowance* (£1,720); lone parents and unmarried couples with children can claim an *additional personal allowance* (also £1,720).

The purpose of married couple's allowance (MCA) and the additional personal allowance (APA) is to protect single-income families against taxation beyond ability to pay. At 25 per cent tax, £1,720 is 'worth' £430 a year, or two weeks' pay for some people. Yet both allowances have been frozen since 1990-91 and are likely to be phased out. Should this happen, single-wage couples will be charged the same income tax as single people with the same income and out-of-work couples could be liable for income tax on the difference between their income support (£71·70 a week) and their income tax allowance (£66·25 a week) – an absurdity which already affects unmarried couples *without children*. According to a Parliamentary Answer by the Treasury to Sir Ralph Howell MP,[17] there is no logical relationship between tax thresholds (which distribute the tax burden) and the income support scale rates (which provide a basic level of subsistence), a reply which identifies Treasury 'logic' as the chief cause of the problem.

If work incentives are to be improved, tax thresholds will have to be raised well clear of income support levels – not just the allowances and premia, but average rents and council tax as well. This is much more important than cutting the standard rate of income tax. Figure 4.5 shows what has happened to tax thresholds since 1950. The distinction between tax thresholds and tax break-even points reflects the switch (in 1977-79) from taxable family allowances and child tax allowances to tax-free child benefit. One reason for the switch was that child tax allowances are worthless to families without the income to set against them, whereas child benefit goes to every child and is recouped from better-off parents through their income tax. The *tax break-even point*[18] has been defined by the Inland Revenue as the earnings level at which income tax paid equals child benefit (or family allowance) received. The decline in break-even points since the mid-1950s is due to the falling away of non-means-tested family income support. Those worst affected are single-wage families with children and large families. A slight improvement during the mid-1980s has not been sustained.

EXAMPLE 1:   In 1950-51 the income tax threshold for a single person was 37 per cent of average male manual earnings. By 1979-80 it had fallen to 23 per cent. It then rose slightly but by April 1994 it was back to 23 per cent. To restore its 1950-51 ratio, it would have to be raised from £66 to £105 a week.

EXAMPLE 2:   In 1950-51 the tax threshold for a single-wage married couple was 60 per cent of average male

---

[17] *Hansard*, 22 February 1995, col.194.

[18] See Glossary, below, p.142.

FIGURE 4.5:
Tax Allowances/Tax Break-Even Points as Percentages of Average Male Manual Earnings, 1950-94

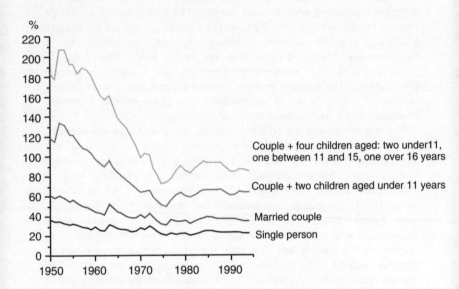

Couple + four children aged: two under 11, one between 11 and 15, one over 16 years

Couple + two children aged under 11 years

Married couple

Single person

Sources: Inland Revenue Statistics 1982 and *Hansard*, Written Answer, 3 February 1994, col. 826.

manual earnings. By 1979-80 it had fallen to 35 per cent. Again it rose slightly thereafter, but by 1994-95 it was back to 35 per cent. To restore its 1950-51 ratio it would have to be raised to £170 a week. Instead it is likely to fall to £66 a week (the same as for a single person).

EXAMPLE 3: In 1950-51 a single-wage couple with two children paid less in income tax than they received in family allowance unless the husband earned 120 per cent of average male manual earnings. By 1979-80 the tax break-even point had fallen to 64 per cent of average male manual earnings, and in 1994-95 it was back at 64 per cent. To restore the 1950-51 position, assuming tax allowances for the parents of £170 a week (Example 2), child benefit would have to be £20 or thereabouts for every child.

Earned-income tax reliefs

Although travel-to-work expenses have never been tax deductible in Britain, earned-income relief was available until 1973. Within the European Union (EU), Britain is exceptional in having virtually no reliefs for the costs regularly associated with paid employment. Even NI contributions and council tax are paid out of taxed income (although NI benefits are taxable). Some EU member-states allow a general earned-income relief *as well as* allowances for specified work expenses. Every fare increase and every increase in petrol duty narrow still further the incentive margins between incomes in and out of work. People are having to travel further to find jobs and some of them have to use their own transport because there is no longer any suitable public transport in the areas where they live.

The costs of childcare

Treasury intransigence on tax relief for work-related childcare is a further reason why social security expenditure is out of control. During the past 12 years, the high cost of childcare for working mothers, its inhibiting effects on labour market participation, and the more advanced provisions available for working mothers elsewhere in Europe have become front-page news.[19] Kilos of evidence have been presented to the Treasury by organisations as far apart as the Institute of Directors, the Equal Opportunities Commission and the National Council for One Parent Families. Yet all that has emerged is the tax exemption of workplace nurseries in the 1990 Finance Act and the £40 childcare disregard with family credit introduced in 1994.

In July 1990 a campaign for Tax Relief and Childcare (TRAC) was launched, with a membership that includes the business community, organisations concerned with childcare and the voluntary sector.[20] TRAC is not asking for increases in public expenditure, it is asking

---

[19] For example: Peter Moss, *Childcare and Equality of Opportunity*, Consolidated Report to the European Commission; and Bronwen Cohen, *Caring for Children*, European Commission, April 1988.

[20] TRAC (The Campaign for Tax Relief and Childcare), *A Strategy for Employer Funded Childcare*, 1991.

for the tax exemption of workplace nurseries introduced in the 1990 Finance Act to be extended to all forms of registered childcare. Although welcome, the impact of tax-exemption workplace nurseries has been limited. If all forms of registered childcare qualified for tax relief, parents whose employers chose not to provide in-house childcare but were prepared to offer childcare vouchers, would be able to make their own arrangements and still qualify for tax relief. By introducing childcare tax relief (within realistic ceilings) the Treasury could reduce benefit expenditure and increase tax revenues simultaneously.

There is, however, another side to the argument. For babies and toddlers, childcare outside the home may not be beneficial. Many mothers forgo earnings in that belief. Rather than channel limited resources into subsidies for childcare, it might be more appropriate to increase child benefit for children under five. That way mothers would be able to choose whether to put the extra benefit towards the costs of childcare or use it as a form of earnings replacement. Any such increase in child benefit could be recouped from better-off families through a more progressive income tax.

(ii) National insurance (NI) contributions

While income tax rates have come down, NI contribution rates have gone up, resulting in a marginal tax rate for most wage earners of 35 per cent, compared with 25 per cent for those whose incomes come through the post, and 40 per cent for top earners. In 1948, when national insurance was introduced, there was a flat-rate 25 pence (5s.) per week contribution for everyone. Although regressive, it represented only 3·7 per cent of average male manual earnings at that time (Figure 4.6). In 1961 an earnings-related component was super-imposed and in 1975 it became entirely earnings-related. Since 1979 the rate for employees not contracted out of the state earnings related pension scheme (SERPS) has gone up from 6·5 per cent to 10 per cent. Although the effects at the bottom of the earnings distribution have been mitigated by adjustments to the rates payable by low earners, almost 2 percentage points have been added to the rate of contribution paid by average earners (Figure 4.6).

(iii) Council tax

For families in the DHSS/DSS Tax Benefit Model Tables, council tax liabilities in 1994/95 were four to five times higher than local auth-

FIGURE 4.6:
National Insurance Contribution as a Percentage of Earnings at Average Male Manual Earnings, 1948-94

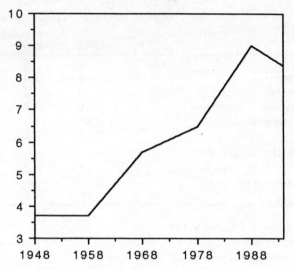

% average male manual earnings

Source: 1948-1988 DSS *Abstract of Statistics*, plus author's calculations.
Note: Post-1975 NI contributions are at not-contracted out rates.

ority rates in 1979/80, compared with three-fold increases in average male manual earnings. Unlike income tax and NI contributions, council tax is not related to income, so the figures in Table 4.2 apply only to families living in local authority housing and paying average local authority rates or council tax. They therefore underestimate the scale of the problem.

EXAMPLE: In 1979, average local authority rates including water rates for a couple with two small children living in local authority housing were £2·30 a week, or 3 per cent of average male manual earnings at that time. By April 1994, average council tax liability for a similar family was £14·40 (including an estimated £3·40 for water rates), or just over 5 per cent of average male manual earnings. *Families on income support do not have to pay council tax. Low earners get at best a rebate.*

TABLE 4.2:
Percentages of Gross Weekly Earnings Taken in Local Authority Tax: DHSS/DSS Model Families, April 1979 and 1994

	At average manual earnings		At two-thirds average manual earnings	
	1979	*1994*	*1979*	*1994*
	%	%	%	%
Single man	3	4	4	5
Single woman	4	6	6	8
Single woman + 2 children	5	6	8	10
Single-wage marrried couple	3	4	4	6
Single-wage couple + 2 children	3	5	5	8
Single-wage couple + 4 children	3	5	5	8

Source: Appendix 1, below, p.127.
Note: For comparability: water rates estimated at £3·40 per week have been included with council tax in 1994.

4. RENTS THROUGH THE ROOF

Since 1979, the cost of shelter has increased faster than any other major component of a typical household budget. During the 1960s a family was said to be 'poor' if it had to spend more than 30 per cent of its income on food. Today, housing is the biggest item of expenditure for many families. In the rented sector, public sector rents have increased six-fold on average since 1979. Figure 4.7 shows how rent increases have contributed to the falling away of work incentives since 1979. Housing association rents have increased even faster and private lettings fastest of all.

EXAMPLE: In 1979-80, the average local authority rent for a two-child family was £6·50 a week, or 7 per cent of average male manual earnings. By 1994-95 the average rent for a similar family was £36·42, or 13 per cent of average male manual earnings. *Families on income support get their rent paid in full, working families get at best a rebate.*

FIGURE 4.7:
Rents Through the Roof
Percentages of earnings taken in local authority rents, at average and two-thirds average male and female manual earnings, DHSS/DSS model families, April 1979 and April 1994

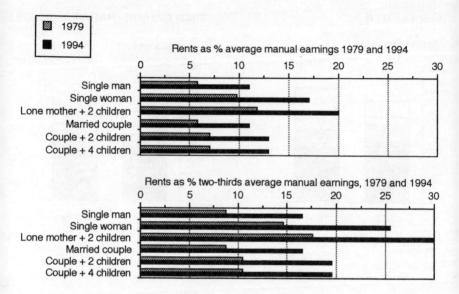

Source: Appendix 1, below, p.127.

5. MIX ALL THESE INGREDIENTS TOGETHER...

Now comes the crunch. Add together the effects on spending power of income tax, NI contributions, council tax and rents, and you have a recipe for the situation Government Ministers complain about: increasing benefit dependency; decline of the traditional family; social disintegration; and mounting crime. Figure 4.8 is based on Appendix 1 (below, pp.127-128). *At the bottom of the earnings distribution (average manual earnings and below), there appear to be few householders for whom incentives to work have improved since 1979. Instead, millions have been lured into dependence upon means-tested welfare, and then castigated for it. The lower their earnings potential and the more numerous their children, the more pronounced those effects have been.*

[continued on p.85]

FIGURE 4.8:
Changes in the Tax and Rent Burden
Percentages of earnings taken in income tax (net of child benefit), NI contribution, local authority rates/council tax, and local authority rents, at average manual earnings, April 1979 and April 1994

SINGLE MAN

% gross earnings

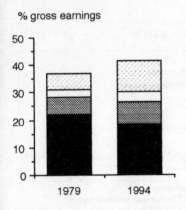

SINGLE-WAGE MARRIED COUPLE

% gross earnings

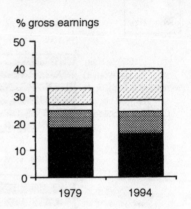

SINGLE-WAGE COUPLE + 2 CHILDREN

% gross earnings

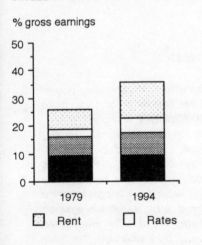

SINGLE-WAGE COUPLE + 4 CHILDREN

% gross earnings

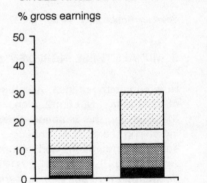

▢ Rent   ▢ Rates   ▨ NI contribution   ◼ Income tax

Source: Appendix 1, below, p.127.

EXAMPLE: In 1994-95, at two-thirds average male manual earnings (£190 per week), a single-wage couple paying average local authority rent and council tax paid 42 per cent of it in direct taxes and rent compared with 31 per cent in 1979.

EXAMPLE: In 1994-95, at two-thirds average female manual earnings (£120 per week), a lone mother with two children paying average local authority rent and council tax paid 29 per cent of her earnings in direct taxes and rent, compared with 6 per cent in 1979.

EXAMPLE: In 1994-95, at average male manual earnings (£281 per week), a married man with two children paying average local authority rent and council tax paid 36 per cent of his earnings in tax and rent, compared with 26 per cent in 1979.

6. ADD A FLAWED SYSTEM OF FAMILY INCOME SUPPORT...

'I doubt', wrote Eleanor Rathbone (campaigner in chief for 'child endowments', or family allowances, during the inter-war years), 'whether there is any subject in the world of equal importance that has received so little serious and articulate consideration as the economic status of the family.'[21] Her criticism remains valid and helps explain the policy failures of the last 16 years. For where ignorance reigns dogma gains easy access – and where dogma reigns informed policy-making is replaced by changes that have not been thought through. Judged by its impact on work incentives and family solidarity, family income support in Britain has five major flaws:

- Child benefit (payable for all children) is so small that it has to be supplemented by means-tested benefits.

- Income tax thresholds for working parents are below their out-of-work benefit entitlements.

- Family credit (payable to low-earners with children) replaces the unemployment trap by the poverty trap.

- The income tax allowance system and the benefit system (especially family credit) are asymmetrical between married couples, unmarried couples and single people.

---

[21] E. Rathbone, *The Disinherited Family, 1924 Family Allowances*, Second Edn., London: Allen and Unwin, 1949, Introduction, p.i.

- For young adults between full-time compulsory school and regular, full-time work, there is a hotch-potch of provisions which do more harm than good.

Despite major reforms to the tax and benefit systems and endless fine-tuning, these problems remain. Instead of using family-friendly and incentive-friendly instruments like child benefit, the preferred options are family-hostile instruments like income support and family credit.

Fragmented benefits for children

As a result of Eleanor Rathbone's campaign for child endowments and his knowledge of pre-war unemployment assistance, Beveridge made family allowances *in time of earning and not earning alike* a key assumption of his Plan:

> 'The gap between income during earning and during interruption of earning should be as large as possible for every man. It cannot be kept large for men with families, except either by making benefit in unemployment and disability inadequate, or by giving allowances for children in time of earning and non-earning alike.'[22]

His advice has gone unheeded. Child support is fragmented across a range of provisions:

- Child benefit (all children);

- One-parent benefit (restricted to lone-parent families);

- Child allowances with income support (restricted to out-of-work families);

- Family credit (restricted to low earners);

- Child additions with long-term NI benefits (in the process of being phased out).

Beveridge recommended family allowances (FAM) for each child after the first averaging 45 pence (9s.) a week (assuming no free school meals). FAM would be taxable, but child tax allowances (at that time the only form of support available to working families) would be retained. As a percentage of average male manual earnings, family allowance at the equivalent of 45 pence (9s.) in 1948 *equates to child benefit at roughly £20 today.* Exclusion by Beveridge of the first child was much criticised, and was eventually

---

[22] Beveridge, 1942, *op. cit.*, para.412.

FIGURE 4.9:
Widening the Child Support Gap:
Child benefit compared with supplementary benefit in April
1979 and income support in April 1994, families with one child,
at April 1994 prices

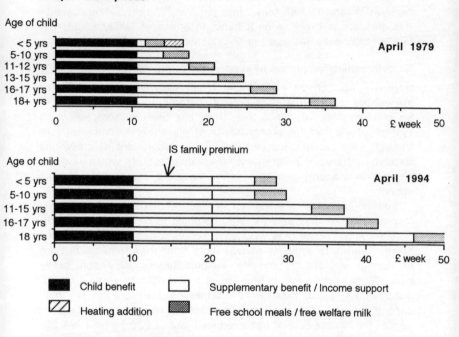

Source: *Social Security Statistics*

changed by the Child Benefit Act of 1975, which replaced child tax
allowances and taxable family allowances with tax-free child
benefits. The chief continuing difficulty has arisen because the war-
time Coalition Government legislated for family allowances of 25
instead of 45 pence, necessitating the payment of additions for
children with the national insurance benefits and national assistance.
When child benefit was introduced, there was talk of increasing it,
to bring it closer to the allowances for children payable with
supplementary benefit. Instead, the gap has widened. In April 1979,
the supplementary benefit (SB) allowance for a child aged under five
was £4·40, compared with child benefit of £4, a gap of only 40
pence. By April 1994, the gap had increased to £9·34 at constant
(1994) prices.

Figure 4.9 shows the high cost of integrating income support
with family credit. This is mainly due to the income support (IS)
family premium (shown in the second graph, to the left of the

vertical lines in the white blocks). As a targeting mechanism the premium is seriously flawed, for it bears no relation to family size or the ages of the children. An unemployed couple with an 18-year-old daughter still at school receives £71·70 for themselves plus a huge £50·24 for their daughter, while a couple with four younger children receives in total £72·65 for all four children. The official response to this criticism is likely to be a hymn in praise of family credit. But family credit does not give families economic independence.

No comprehensive system of support for young adults

Until the replacement of (taxable) family allowances and child tax allowances by tax-free child benefit, parents could claim tax relief for children over 16. Since then there has been no comprehensive system of support for young adults at all, either independently or through their parents. Instead there is an assortment of provisions through different Government Departments, of which income support is the only one that offers anything approaching income security.

Sixteen-year-olds staying on at school remain the financial responsibility of their parents, who continue to receive child benefit. Sixteen- and 17-year-olds who leave school forfeit the right to child benefit, count as separate benefit units from their families, but are no longer entitled to income support unless they can prove exceptional need. Every school leaver has a right to youth training, but the training may be delayed and may not lead to a job, in which case they may be penniless. On reaching age 18, they become eligible for income support, at a reduced rate of £36·15 (in 1994-95) a week. Although a number of government-sponsored training programmes exists, these are intended for the long-term unemployed. Young people made redundant who purchase their own training, disqualify themselves from income support. It is the most enormous muddle. *What is needed is a system which will keep 16-25-year-olds out of poverty while making sure that they study, train or take paid work.*

Chipping away at the traditional family

Whether or not one takes a moral view about lone-parent families, there is no doubt that under present arrangements they impose a costly burden on the rest of society – hence reason enough, from an economist's point of view, for changes that will strengthen the traditional, two-parent family.

Strong families are so important to economic prosperity that where the balance of advantage has to go one way or another, there is an economic case for leaning in favour of two-parent rather than one-parent families. Instead, successive governments have chipped away at the traditional two-parent, single-earner family: they have hit families hard with extra tax; cut back on child benefit; and generally made non-earners (particularly non-earning mothers) feel inferior.

This urge to get every man and every woman into the labour market has nothing to do with women's emancipation, which is about freedom of choice, but has more to do with an outdated socialism, which sees everybody's salvation in the labour market. The removal of the married couple's tax allowance, unless replaced by something better (for instance, convertible tax credits or basic incomes), will weaken family life during stages of the life cycle (child-bearing, child-rearing, disability and old age) when families are most vulnerable.

By 1994-95, at average male earnings of £374 a week, the net income[23] of a man with a non-earning wife and two children was only £23 more than the net income of a single person.[24]

Marriage as the DSS sees it

A Government seriously intent upon strengthening legal marriage would start by using a consistent definition of it. For Inland Revenue purposes marriage still means what most people think it means: a mutual commitment that is binding unless legally dissolved. But for DSS purposes a married couple is defined as 'a man and woman who are married to each other *and are members of the same household*', and an unmarried couple as 'a man and woman who are not married to each other but are living together as husband and wife otherwise than in prescribed circumstances'.[25] While an absconding spouse no longer counts as married, a lone mother applying for family credit has to get her new 'partner' to fill in one-half of the Family Credit form, and thereby take financial responsibility for a child whose natural father is perhaps being pursued by the Child Support Agency. In cases of cohabitation the Benefits Agency decides whether or not a couple are 'living together as husband and wife' (the much-hated *cohabitation rule*), but two men or two women sharing accommodation automatically count as separate benefit units regardless of their sexual relationship!

Penalties for marriage in the benefit system

In 1994-95 the income support rate for a married couple was £71·70, compared with £45·70 for a single person from age 25 (householders and non-householders alike) – so the implied 'cost of

---

23 See Glossary, below, p.137.

24 *Hansard*, Written Answer, 19 January 1994, cols. 639-42.

25 *Social Security Bill 1986*, Part 2, p.21.

TABLE 4.3:
Why Marry? Penalties for Marriage in the Benefit System, April 1994-95. £ per week

A. INCOME SUPPORT (IS)	IS allowances and premiums	Total benefit	Child or separation bonus
	£	£	£
1. Single person 18-24 yrs.	36·15	36·15	
2. Single person + 1 child	76·50	76·50	40·35
3. Couple + 1 child	97·40	97·40	
4. Dad moves out:			
Mother + 1 child	76·50)		
	)	122·20	24·80
Dad	45·70)		

B. FAMILY CREDIT	Net spending power from gross weekly earnings of:		
	£100	£150	£200
Couple + 2 children	129	131	136
Single person + 2 children	133	135	145

Source: Hansard, Written Answer, 18 October 1993, cols. 166-67.

a wife' was £26, even if she was pregnant. In the same year, an unemployed couple with a baby got £97·40 for all three of them, while a lone mother with a baby got £76·50 – so here the implied 'cost of a wife' is £20·90. The figures in Table 4.3 should not be taken to imply that large numbers of teenage girls use pregnancy as a way of obtaining the dole, or that couples on income support easily take the decision to live apart. They are shown here to illustrate the idiocies of the system. Family credit (shown in Part B of Table 4.3) produces even stranger anomalies. *Lone mothers on family credit obtain more spending power from a given wage than two-parent families with the same number of children.* No wonder Alan Marsh and Stephen McKay found family credit more popular with lone parents than couples.[26]

---

[26] Marsh and McKay, *op. cit.* The take-up rate in 1991 was 78 per cent for lone parents, 60 per cent for couples.

7. ...AND YOU HAVE A NEW BYZANTIUM

In 1984, I described the UK benefit system as incomprehensible, uncoordinated and unnecessarily expensive to administer.[27] Today it may be better co-ordinated, but it is less comprehensible and even more expensive to administer. Administrative costs were £4,300 million in 1993-94 compared with £2,500 million in 1988-89 (when the Fowler reforms were introduced), and the number of staff involved was 99,000 in 1993-94, compared with 90,000 in 1988-89.[28] High administrative costs are a characteristic of all means-tested and work-tested benefit systems. By 1992-93 administrative costs as percentages of benefit expenditure ranged from 1.2 per cent for NI retirement pensions to 10.4 per cent for income support, 15.3 per cent for unemployment benefit and a colossal 51.7 per cent for the Social Fund.[29]

Membership of Britain's new Byzantium includes the Department of Social Security and the Treasury (founder members), plus the Departments of Employment, Education and Environment, plus the local authorities. Since 1979 the DSS and the Department of Employment have introduced so many new schemes and changed their marketing jargon so many times that even the 'experts' are aghast. Claimants, especially first-time claimants, are bewildered. Some give up. Others learn to milk the system.

*   *   *

With modern technology none of this is necessary. The way to remove Byzantium is to remove the need for case work. And the way to remove the need for case work is by reducing dependence on work-tested and means-tested benefits.

---

[27] Hermione Parker, *Action on Welfare*, London: Social Affairs Unit, 1984, p.7.

[28] Department of Social Security, *The Government's Expenditure Plans, 1994-95 to 1996-97*, Cm. 2513, London: HMSO, 1994, Table 9, p.85, and Figure 34, p.48.

[29] Cm.2513, *ibid.*, Figure 29, p.46.

PART FIVE

There Is an Alternative

1. MORE CARROT, LESS STICK

At the bottom of the income distribution, widespread erosion of incentives to work and to save alongside a weakening of family life have not been remedied by the tax and benefit changes of the past 15 years. Instead, the situation has deteriorated. It is a problem that needs to be tackled from several directions at once, with the emphasis on poverty prevention (helping people to help themselves) rather than poverty relief (removing its symptoms), and an operational strategy that includes the following:

- Lifting the lower paid out of tax.

- Abolition of NI contributions.

- Increases in non-means-tested family income support.

- Symmetry between married and single.

- Study and training allowances which take priority over the dole.

- A moratorium on rent increases.

2. CRITERIA

To achieve these goals the first priority is a set of criteria against which every policy proposal can be judged, such as the following:

- Simplicity,

- Privacy,

- Adequacy,

- Symmetry,

- Economic efficiency.

Simplicity

Simplicity should be judged from the point of view of taxpayers and beneficiaries, as well as administrators. As a result of chip technology, social policy is becoming a numbers game. Reform options churned out by computers disregard administrative difficulties and consumer preferences. People are being squeezed out, and know it. During the early 1980s, as the DSS case-load soared, simplicity became so confused with automation that automation became an end in itself, and the fundamental question *WHY* the case load was out of control was ignored.

The 1988 social security reforms may have rationalised the benefit system from the point of view of administrators, but they left claimants bemused. For them, simplification means benefit amounts that are crystal clear, regulations that match the lives they live and allow them to fulfil their aspirations, ease of access, low compliance costs, the minimum of intrusion and continuity. Individual assessment units are preferable to family-based units for taxpayers and claimants. Any system that takes the income of both spouses (or 'partners') into account introduces complexity. For administrators, real simplification means tax and benefit systems the bulk of which can be automated without loss of control, or fear of abuse. Work tests, 'participation' tests, means tests, family-based tax or benefit units all add to case work. Fraud and abuse correlate with high compliance costs. There must be computerisation, but where compliance costs are high computers cannot replace experienced case officers.

For these reasons any reform proposal that increases dependence on means-tested or work-tested benefits, or takes families as the assessment unit, scores low on the simplicity rating.

Privacy

In a democracy privacy should be a right of citizenship. One reason the DSS cohabitation rule is so unpopular (and difficult to operate) is the invasion of privacy it entails. The right to privacy should become part of the Citizen's Charter, and should start with government. It is unacceptable that people should be required to answer questions about the most intimate details of their lives in order to qualify for (or be disqualified from) benefit.

For these reasons any proposal that involves increased reliance on family-based assessment units scores low on the privacy rating.

Adequacy

A rational income transfer system (taxes as well as benefits) would start from estimates of needs and costs, obtained using the *budget standards* methodology pioneered by Seebohm Rowntree in 1901,[1] and modified by the *Family Budget Unit* in 1992.[2] Without such estimates, governments are targeting blindfold. Budget standards are specified baskets of goods and services which, when priced, represent pre-defined living standards. The contents of the 'baskets' are not set in stone; rather they are benchmarks. Those selected by the Family Budget Unit are based on scientifically assessed estimates of nutritional and other needs, modified by study of consumer preferences and tests of public opinion. The living standard generally regarded as most valuable is what Americans call *modest-but-adequate (MBA)* and Scandinavians call *reasonable*. First used in 1948 by the United States Bureau of Labor Statistics, the MBA level aims to 'satisfy prevailing standards of what is necessary for health, efficiency, the nurture of children and participation in community activities'. At roughly twice the poverty level, it allows families to run a second-hand car, take an annual holiday and avoid debt problems, but is well below affluence. By adapting the MBA budgets, or starting afresh, it is also possible to produce low-cost budgets suitable for social security benefit scales. However, this is more difficult because low-cost budgets, due to their smaller margins, depend on the length of time families are expected to live on them; and on rent, travel-to-work costs and other circumstances over which most families have little control.

Summary MBA budgets for six model families are in Appendix 4 (below, p.131). Figure 5.1 shows how the components of each family's budget build up. In 1993-94, a two-earner couple with two children aged 4 and 10, living in local authority housing in York, had to spend £330 a week to reach the Family Budget Unit's MBA standard, compared with £220 for a married couple and £160 for a single man. Grossed up for NI contribution and income tax (less child benefit), the couple with children needed gross earnings of £400 a week (£20,450 a year), compared with £250 a week (£13,000 a year) for the married couple and £210 a week (£10,800 a year) for the single man.

---

[1] Seebohm Rowntree, *op. cit.*

[2] The Family Budget Unit Ltd is a small educational charity, currently based at King's College, London. For an explanation of the methods used, see Jonathan Bradshaw (ed.), *Budget Standards for the United Kingdom*, Aldershot: Avebury, 1993.

FIGURE 5.1:
Estimated Spending and Earnings Needed to Reach a Modest-but-Adequate Living Standard, October 1993

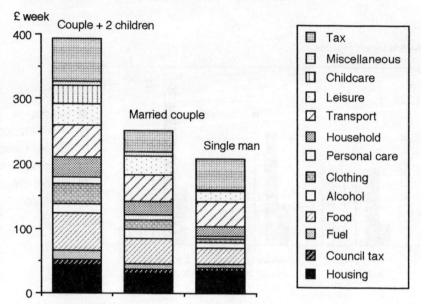

Source: Family Budget Unit Ltd, 1994.

In some countries, budget standards are used to calculate the *equivalence ratios*[3] necessary for families of different composition to reach approximate living standard equivalence and are found to be particularly useful in reference to social security benefit rates, income tax allowances and the thresholds for graduated income tax. In Britain there is a well of ignorance so deep that few people are even aware of the existence of these ratios. In proposing that families pay tax on their child benefits if the income of either parent reaches the higher-rate tax threshold, the Labour Party's Commission on Social Justice implied that a single threshold (£23,700) provides the same living standard for families of all shapes and sizes.[4] Yet according to Family Budget Unit estimates, £23,700 provides twice the MBA standard for a single man, but only just above it for a family with two children.

Using DSS equivalence scales, the indications are that child benefit is much better targeted than is generally supposed. To con-

---

[3]   See Glossary, below, p.144.

[4]   Commission on Social Justice, *op. cit.*, p.316.

FIGURE 5.2:
Distribution of Child Benefit Expenditure by Income Bands of Recipient Families: GB, 1990 and 1991

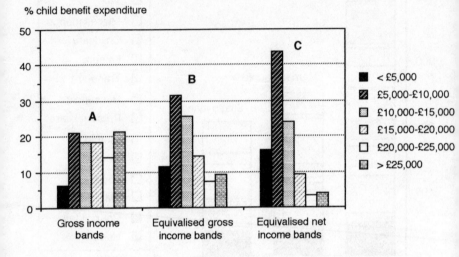

Source: Hansard, Written Answer, 2 December 1993, cols. 721-22.

vert the crude measure of child benefit expenditure (Section A of Figure 5.2) into figures that take account of family composition (Section B), the DSS statisticians divide gross family incomes by the equivalence ratios used in their *Households Below Average Income* statistics.[5] The DSS ratios probably underestimate need at the bottom of the income distribution.[6] Nevertheless, once tax is also taken into account (Section C), it becomes apparent that only 4 per cent of child benefit expenditure in 1991 went to families with equivalised net incomes of over £25,000.

For reasons such as these, tax and benefit proposals that are not accompanied by figures showing the household budget assumptions behind them should score low on the adequacy rating.

---

5   DSS, *Households below average incomes*, 1994, *op. cit.*: see Appendix 4, below, p.131.

6   Because they rely entirely on the Family Expenditure Survey, there is a tacit assumption that what low-income households spend is also what they need.

Symmetry

In an ideal world, tax and benefit policies would be symmetrical between men and women, married and single. In practice, symmetry is not always compatible with adequacy, so compromises have to be made. In Britain, the present structure of income tax allowances penalises single-wage couples, especially unmarried couples (who pay the same tax as single people, see Table 5.1), whilst favouring two-earner married couples and two-earner unmarried couples with children (who get two personal allowances *plus* a married couple's allowance (MCA) or equivalent). The solution currently favoured by all the main political parties is to abolish MCA, but this would leave single-earner couples even more disadvantaged than at present. There is a real dilemma here, which most OECD countries tackle by providing income tax reliefs or cash transfers for non-earning spouses.[7]

Britain looks set to become the odd one out. Offsetting the extra income tax payable by increasing child benefit, as proposed by Labour and the Liberal Democrats, is wide of the mark, because non-earning adults (with or without children) must also eat to survive. The only reform option currently available likely to solve this dilemma is a basic income (below, pp.98-102), because everyone would receive it (including non-earners) either as a tax credit or as a cash benefit.

For this reason, basic income is the only reform option currently available that scores high on the symmetry rating.

TABLE 5.1:
Lack of Symmetry: UK Income Tax, 1994-95

	Income tax allowance ratios to single person		
	Existing	No MCA	Basic income
Single earner	1·0	1·0	1·0
Two-earner married couple	2·4*	2·0	2·0
Two-earner unmarried couple	2·0	2·0	2·0
Single-earner married couple	1·4*	1·0	2·0
Single-earner unmarried couple	1·0	1·0	2·0

* Married couple's allowance (MCA) restricted to 20% tax.

7   OECD, *The Tax/Benefit postion of production workers*, Annual Report 1990-1993, Paris: OECD, 1994.

Economic efficiency

For the purposes of this inquiry, economic efficiency is defined in terms of incentives to work and to save, and good targeting. Regarding the latter, a government seriously intent upon getting unemployed families back to work would pay more attention to tax break-even points.[8] Since the early 1980s a campaign of increasing ferocity has been waged against universal and contributory benefits, on the grounds that they are 'poorly targeted'. Meanwhile another, equally vigorous campaign has been waged to cut income tax rates, *even though this reduces the targeting efficiency of the benefit system.*

Provided break-even points are not too high, universal benefits score higher on the economic efficiency ratings than means-tested benefits, because they sharpen incentives. Instead, the reduction in income tax rates is pushing tax break-even points to all-time highs. For example, using a 30 per cent tax rate, retirement pension at £57·60 is offset by the time taxable income (including the state basic pension) reaches £192 a week – compared with £288 a week using a 20 per cent tax rate. Similarly, child benefit at £10·20 is offset by the time the parents' joint taxable income reaches £34 a week using a 30 per cent tax rate, compared with £50 a week using a 20 per cent tax rate. Put another way, if income tax were at 35 per cent, child benefit could be £17·50 and still be offset by the time the parents' joint taxable income reached £50 a week.

Taxation and benefits are like the two sides of a coin. Nobody wants to return to the high income tax rates of the 1970s, but an understanding of the interaction between the tax and benefit systems would allow family income support to be more effectively targeted and dependence on means-tested benefits greatly reduced.

For such reasons, economic efficiency has to be judged in terms of the tax and benefit systems taken together, not one at a time. An integrated tax-benefit system with income tax rates geared to withdraw benefit at pre-defined living standards could combine adequacy, symmetry and economic efficiency.

3. INTEGRATION OF THE TAX AND BENEFIT SYSTEMS

A further question is how to improve the coherence of policy-making. Many people would reply that government is of its nature incoherent, therefore the less government the less the incoherence. Partly for this reason the rest of this *Research Monograph* will concentrate on a reform option called *Citizen's Income (CI)*,[9] or more precisely the variant of it called *Basic Income (BI)*.[10] BI is

---

8   Defined as the point at which benefits received equal income tax paid.

9   See Glossary, below, p.145.

10   See Glossary, below, p.143.

descended directly from the proposals put forward by Juliet Rhys Williams, as an alternative to the Beveridge Plan. BI would simplify the tax and benefit systems and take government off the backs of the people. For most people the BIs would be flat-rate credits against their income tax, age-related but with no differences on account of gender, work status or marital status. For people with no incomes or with incomes below the BI amounts, however, the BIs would convert automatically into cash benefits upon which they would be free to build through paid work, without having to sign on or off, without being dubbed 'scroungers' and without having to subject themselves to a cohabitation test.

Take a simple example. This year's personal income tax allowance is worth £27 a week to higher-rate taxpayers, £16·95 to standard-rate taxpayers, £13·50 to starting-rate taxpayers and nothing at all to people without the income to set against it. With basic income, it would be worth the same to everyone, either as a tax deduction or a cash credit.

A modified BI (that is to say, a BI which includes an element of income-testing) is the only reform option currently on the agenda which would be likely to meet the requirements set out at the start of this chapter.

Full basic income and partial basic income

BI is no panacea. It could not deal with the housing morass nor provide young people with the training they require. But it would be a monumental step in the right direction. Its efficacy, however, as with any form of social security, would depend on getting the right balance between the BI amounts and the tax rates necessary to finance them. That is why, in the literature about BI, a distinction is drawn between *full basic income* and *partial basic income*. With full BI every legal resident gets a BI that is 'sufficient to live on', whilst paying tax on all (or almost all) their other income, and with no other benefits available. The tax rate depends on the BI amounts and the size of the income tax base, but is unlikely to be less than 50 per cent given the present scale of state social subsidies in Britain.

A major difficulty is to know how much income is enough to live on. Although budget standards research suggests that most people (after allowing for differences in age, household composition and labour market participation) have similar basic needs, housing costs are notoriously variable, so for most families a full BI would provide either too much or too little. That is why people who have studied BI usually conclude that a partial BI (defined as 'not enough to live on'), combined with an income-tested housing benefit and/or a partial negative income tax (NIT), is preferable.

Basic income guarantee (BIG)

Many partial BI variants have been put forward. The first to be costed were the Tax Credit proposals of 1972,[11] which would prob-

---

[11] Treasury and DHSS, *Proposals for a Tax-Credit System, op. cit.*

FIGURE 5.3:
Anatomy of a 'BIG' Scheme

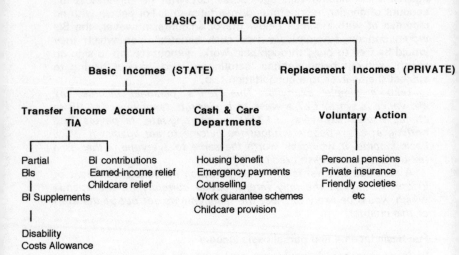

ably have become law but for the 1974 General Election. Also in 1972, in a classic essay, James Meade set out the case for a partial BI combined with a partial NIT.[12] During the 1980s, I worked with Sir Brandon Rhys Williams, MP, on a partial BI strategy which he called his *Basic Income Guarantee* (BIG).[13] This is neither a socialist nor a libertarian dream, but a compromise. Government involvement in income maintenance is limited to the safety net. Those desiring a given percentage of previous earnings during sickness, unemployment or old age are expected to make the necessary provision through private insurance and/or collective agreements (Figure 5.3).

---

12 James Meade, 'Poverty and the Welfare State', *Oxford Economic Papers*, Vol. 24, No.3, Clarendon Press, Oxford, 1972. Although Meade used the term 'social dividend' instead of basic income, the argument is the same.

13 Brandon Rhys Williams, *Stepping Stones to Independence: National Insurance after 1990*, ed. Hermione Parker, Aberdeen University Press, 1989. The first official use of the term Basic Income in the UK was in evidence submitted by Sir Brandon to a Sub Committee of the House of Commons Treasury Select Committee in July 1982. (House of Commons, Treasury and Civil Service Committee Sub-Committee, Session 1982-83, *Minutes of Evidence*, London: HMSO, May 1983.)

Whilst it is theoretically possible to devise any number of BIG schemes, the underlying strategy is always the same. Poverty is tackled by replacing the dole with an income guarantee that is not conditional upon not working, at the same time strengthening the traditional two-parent family. The problem of the married couple's income tax allowance is overcome by giving every man and woman a tax credit that converts into cash if they have no (or insufficient) income to set against it. Poverty can be prevented and symmetry achieved using a single policy instrument (Table 5.1). 'BIG' would protect lone parents and help them regain their financial independence,[14] but it would also remove the present subsidies for marriage break-up (Table 4.4). Everybody would get the partial BI. Elderly people, people with disabilities and certain categories of carers would get BI supplements as well. But the old-age supplement would be related to length of residence in the UK.[15]

At local level the British tradition of separating 'cash' services from 'care' services is not always good value for money. A unified system would make it easier for local authorities and voluntary organisations to tackle 'poverty' at its roots, using positive discretion. Hence the proposal shown in Figure 5.3 for new, integrated 'Cash and Care' departments. Together with the BIs (but not without them) a change of this sort could become a catalyst for positive discretion at community level. Clearly it would require extensive consultation, but the idea behind it is to help people to become financially independent instead of simply doling out money. It therefore coincides with the thinking behind France's *revenu minimum d'insertion (RMI)*, introduced in 1988. In return for the RMI (or minimum participation income), claimants must sign a *contrat d'insertion*, by which they undertake to accept whatever work, training or other initiatives are required of them. Introduced in 1988, the RMI has encountered many difficulties and is not available to people below age 25. Yet there is a wisdom behind it which says that 'poverty', especially deep-seated 'poverty', cannot be remedied by cash benefits alone.

The problems are political

Research carried out since the 1980s, mainly at the London School of Economics, indicates that partial BI is economically feasible, but

---

[14] H. Parker (ed.), *Citizen's Income and Women*, BIRG Discussion Paper No. 2, Citizen's Income Study Centre, 1993. BI on its own cannot solve the lone-parent trap. Other measures, including maintenance allowances, childcare tax reliefs and childcare vouchers are also necessary.

[15] In Denmark, 40 years' residence is required to qualify for a full citizen's pension.

should start at a low rate. Opposition to it is largely political, especially worries about the work ethic and (for some people) the redistribution of income it would involve from men to women.[16] Certainly it cannot happen without agreement between the political parties. If poverty is to be avoided, some selectivity will always be necessary, but this can be done by giving more to certain 'demogrant' groups (e.g. children, pensioners or people with disabilities) and by use of income tests rather than means tests. For the danger with all forms of poverty relief – and giving them fancy names makes not one jot of difference – is that unless the accompanying regulations are harsh (and administratively burdensome), dependence upon them grows like topsy, a fact which has been well known since Speenhamland[17] and which we ignore at our peril.

The choice, therefore, is not between an integrated tax-benefit system and the existing system, it is between an integrated system, an increasingly harsh version of the existing system, and an elaborated version of national insurance accompanied by ever-increasing unemployment.

4. REFORM OPTIONS: KEY DIFFERENCES

Figure 5.4 summarises the social security options currently on the agenda. Traditional social security systems are shown on the left, CI systems are on the right. CI is a broad church whose main variables are the basis of entitlement, the unit of assessment and the financing method.

Basis of entitlement: *work or legal residence?*

Work status benefits are products of the industrial revolution, CIs are products of the 'post-industrial' revolution and women's emancipation. Although work status benefits still dominate, they are increasingly called in question. What is needed, so the argument goes, is a redefinition of work which puts a 'tab' on the value of unpaid work. For although hard to measure, some unpaid work ('women's work') is as economically and socially valuable as some paid work. Due to women's emancipation, new family forms and increasing family breakdown, it would be unwise to assume that women will always be content to jeopardise their well-being in old

---

[16] H. Parker (ed.), *op. cit.*

[17] In 1795, under what came to be known as the Speenhamland System, poor relief was indexed to the price of bread and included supplements for each child, including illegitimate children.

FIGURE 5.4:
Income Maintenance Family Tree

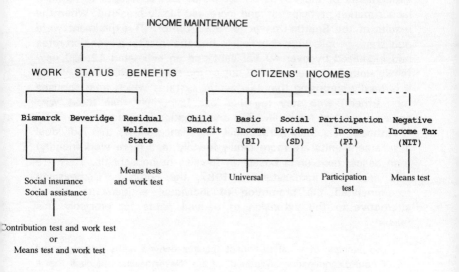

age by putting their caring responsibilities ahead of their economic self-interest.[18]

Many women are in a dilemma. Responsible parenthood means putting their children first, filial affection means putting elderly parents first, and because men earn more than women, it is usually the women's jobs that go. With either a New Beveridge or a residual welfare state, the balance is likely to shift in favour of paid work regardless. Mothers will pay other mothers to look after their children, more old people and more sick people will be hived off into institutions, and more men will be jobless.

Assessment unit: *families or individuals?*

With social insurance, national insurance and most CI proposals, but not negative income tax (NIT), the assessment unit is the individual, whether married or single. With means-tested and income-tested benefits (including NIT), it is the 'family' or 'household'. In Britain it

---

[18] NI contribution credits for non-earning mothers count only towards the state basic pension, which will be worthless by the time most of them reach pension age, because it is indexed to prices not earnings. For further discussion see Hermione Parker (ed.), *op. cit.*

is the one-generational family, elsewhere in Europe it may be the two- or three-generational family, or wider family unit. Although family-based units are theoretically more cost-effective, the NIT experiments of the 1970s showed they can contribute to reduced labour-market participation and increased family break-up. When the results of the Seattle-Denver (or SIME-DIME) NIT experiment were published, people were shocked to find that marital dissolution rates had increased by over 40 per cent and an estimated 12,000 new family units had been created out of the original 4,800 units.[19] Yet it is hardly surprising that tax-benefit systems which treat spouses (or partners) who stay together less favourably than those who separate weaken family life. The only question is by how much.

Although it sounds paradoxical, experience shows that individual assessment units are more family-friendly (and more work-friendly) than assessment units based on families or households. They are also easier to administer. In 1987, the European Commission recommended the promotion of individual entitlements as an alternative to the extension of derived rights for precisely this reason:

> 'The principle of equal treatment requires derived rights to be granted without discrimination on grounds of sex. Nevertheless, it is clear that a breach of the marital relationship could endanger the very existence of derived rights and that for this reason a system of *personal rights* provides better guarantees for the social protection of spouses.'[20]

Financing methods and the tax base

Most existing social security systems rely on a mixture of social (or national) insurance contributions and general taxation. BI would use an integrated income tax. Social dividend is more often perceived as a share of profits. NIT systems use income tax but it cannot be integrated, because different administrative regulations apply above and below the break-even levels at which positive tax becomes payable. NI contributions have so far been less unpopular than income tax, because contributors (wrongly) suppose they are good

---

19 SRI International, *Final Report of the Seattle-Denver Income Maintenance Experiment*, Vol.1: *Design and Results*, p.365; G. Christophersen, Vol.2: *Administration, Mathematical Policy Research*, US Government Printing Office, 1983, p.163.

20 'Proposals for a COUNCIL DIRECTIVE completing the implementation of the principle of equal treatment for men and women in statutory and occupational social security schemes', Commission of the European Communities, COM(87) 494 final, 9466/87, Brussels: CEC, 1987, p.7 (my emphasis).

value for money. They would, of course, be inappropriate with CI, to which everybody would be entitled. An integrated income tax would raise more revenue than a work-based tax and remove anomalies.

Most BI proposals scrap all NI contributions, all income tax allowances and some or all income tax reliefs (for example, for mortgage interest and private pensions). Some proposals sharpen incentives by including earned-income tax credits and tax relief for childcare costs. Public support for the insurance concept suggests that by calling the new income tax a *basic income contribution* and hypothecating it to an independently operated Transfer Income Account, the scheme is more likely to win electoral support. But this proposal does assume that the rest of public expenditure can be financed through other taxes, including the revenue from whatever tax replaced employers' NI contributions.

5. CITIZEN'S INCOME VARIANTS

Returning to the CI variants in Figure 5.4, the aim is to ensure that the carrot (CI plus wages net of tax) is sufficiently tempting to start a virtuous circle of rising output and tax revenues. Some variants would do this more effectively than others, yet none on its own can solve all the problems described in this *Research Monograph*. Almost certainly, the optimum solution will require a judicious blend of universal, income-tested and 'participation' benefits. The universal element could be in the form of a partial BI, with or without social dividend; the income-tested element might be in the form of an income-tested housing benefit, with or without a partial NIT; while the 'participation' requirement could be general or limited to certain age groups, or linked to housing benefit.

Child benefit and residence-based old age pensions

First introduced in Britain in 1977, as a replacement for taxable family allowances and child tax allowances, child benefit is a BI for children – payable universally and at the same rates whether or not the parents are in paid work. Because it is payable for all children, it carries no stigma, is easy to understand, inexpensive to administer and has a take-up rate of virtually 100 per cent. In a public attitudes survey carried out by Gallup Poll as part of Sir Norman Fowler's Social Security Review, 80 per cent of child benefit recipients were in favour of it.[21] Most OECD countries have similar provisions. Less usual but of equal relevance are the residence-based pensions payable in the Netherlands, Scandinavia and Canada. All are *de facto* citizen's pensions.

---

[21] *Reform of Social Security, Background Papers*, Vol.3, Cmnd.9519, London: HMSO, 1985.

Transitional basic income (TBI)

Full BI and partial BI have already been explained. Both descend from Juliet Rhys Williams via Richard Titmuss's *Three Worlds of Welfare*,[22] the 1972 Tax-Credit proposals,[23] the writings of James Meade[24] and the work of Juliet Rhys Williams's son, the late Sir Brandon Rhys Williams.[25] Partial BI is one of the most forward-looking yet practical reform options currently on the agenda – the difficulty is to get from here to there. However, recent research suggests that BIs of £15-£20 a week, combined with other measures, could set in motion the required virtuous circle of increasing economic activity and tax revenues. Such BIs are called 'transitional' BIs or TBIs.

They are transitional because their purpose is to build a bridge between the existing tax and benefit systems and a new, partially integrated system. Because of the need to avoid unacceptable tax increases or sudden civil service job losses, any move towards BI has to be gradual, yet the TBIs must also be sufficient to begin the long process of lifting people out of dependence on work-tested and means-tested benefits. Micro-simulation models show surprisingly large gains at the bottom of the income distribution from quite small TBIs. At the top there would be tax increases (assuming a revenue-neutral change), but in the long term all should gain from the increased rates of sustainable economic growth. TBI is so important that two costed TBI options will be explained in Section 7 of this chapter (below, pp.111-118).

Social dividend and 'topsy-turvy nationalisation'

Unlike BI, social dividend would be financed out of company profits, not as a tax but as a dividend. Otherwise the two are similar. Although less researched than BI, the history of social dividend is much longer, going back at least as far as Thomas Paine, who argued that every individual has a legitimate claim to a share in the 'natural property...which comes to us from the creator of the universe – such as the earth, air, water'.[26] Social dividend can also

---

22 Richard Titmuss, 'The Social Division of Welfare', in *Essays on the Welfare State*, London: Allen & Unwin, 1958.

23 Treasury and DHSS, *op. cit.*, 1972.

24 James Meade, *op. cit.*, 1972; also his *Liberty, Equality and Efficiency*, London: Macmillan, 1993.

25 Brandon Rhys Williams (H. Parker (ed.)), *op. cit.*, 1989.

26 Thomas Paine, *Agrarian Justice* (1797).

boast one fully operative scheme, for in the State of Alaska a part of the profits from oil extracted at Prudhoe Bay has been redistributed annually to every man, woman and child since 1982. The origins of the programme go back to 1976 when Governor Jay Hammond used the term 'Alaska Incorporated' to spread the idea that Alaskans should be treated as stockholders in a corporation (the State of Alaska) that was extracting oil at Prudhoe Bay. Economic analysis shows beneficial results, including increased total personal incomes and higher levels of economic activity, even during recession.[27]

Working independently, James Meade's proposals for 'topsy-turvy nationalisation' strike a similar note. In recent years Meade has proposed that governments should cease to manage any of their countries' national assets, which should instead be run by privately managed, competitive investment trusts, with a share of the profits distributed annually amongst the populace.[28] Like Charles Handy[29] and others, Meade looks forward to the day when every Briton will have a portfolio of incomes, including dividends, income from savings and state transfers as well as wages or salaries.

Samuel Brittan carries the argument further. Citizen's income (CI), he says, should be seen 'not as a handout, but as a property right'.[30] Whilst recognising the importance of a national minimum that is adequate and a tax-benefit system that does not undermine incentives, Brittan argues for the right of every citizen in a free society to 'opt out' if they wish to. For Brittan, CI is a way of separating the libertarian, free-choice aspects of capitalism from the puritan work ethic, giving every citizen the freedom of choice at present restricted to a minority. 'The only thing wrong with unearned income', says Brittan, 'is that too few have it.'[31]

This debate, and the Alaskan experience, are immensely relevant to the future of the welfare state. Meade, Handy, Brittan and others

---

[27] J. Patrick O'Brien and Dennis O. Olsen, *The Alaska Permanent Fund and Dividend Distribution Programme*, BIRG Bulletin No.12, January 1991, Citizen's Income Study Centre, St. Philips Building, Sheffield Street, London WC2A 2EX.

[28] James Meade, *Liberty, Equality and Efficiency*, London: Macmillan, 1993, pp.94-96.

[29] Charles Handy, *The Age of Unreason*, London: Hutchinson 1989, Arrow paperback, 1990.

[30] Samuel Brittan and Steven Webb, *Beyond the Welfare State: An Examinationof Basic Incomes in a Market Economy*, The David Hume Institute, Aberdeen University Press, 1990, p.3.

[31] Brittan and Webb, *ibid.*, p.4.

are arguing for an income guarantee that will increase choice – as well as providing income security. *But it cannot happen in a means-tested, work-tested, welfare state.*

'Participation' income (PI)

Unfortunately, the world is composed of authoritarians as well as libertarians. Authoritarians do not trust other people's choices, they think they know better. Somewhere along the line, they say, there has to be a mechanism that will sort out the sheep from the goats, in the form of a work test. Tony Atkinson's *participation income* (PI) can best be seen as a compromise between the libertarian and authoritarian positions. In two public lectures in December 1992, first at the London School of Economics and then at a Plenary Session of the European Poverty Summit at Edinburgh, Atkinson argued that Europe should retain but 'modernise its social insurance systems and also develop a BI conditional upon "participation"'.[32] Atkinson's PI would be payable to all who complied with the participation requirements, defined roughly as anyone in paid work or available for work, sick or disabled, students and trainees, mothers with dependent children, people caring for young, elderly or disabled dependants, and people undertaking approved forms of voluntary work. By definition, however, some people would get neither a PI nor an income tax allowance.

In making this proposal, Atkinson follows in the tracks of Juliet Rhys Williams, who proposed a social contract between the individual and the state,

> 'whereby the State would acknowledge the duty to maintain the individual and his children at all times and... the individual, in his turn, would acknowledge it to be his duty to devote his best efforts to the production of the wealth whereby alone the welfare of the community can be maintained.'[33]

The justification, for both of them, is that without some sort of conditionality, support for BI will be too limited. It is a strong argument, but PI is not the only answer to it. On the contrary, given that administrative simplicity is one of BI's main attractions, why

---

[32] A.B. Atkinson, *Beveridge, the National Minimum, and its Future in a European Context*, Discussion Paper WSP/85, Suntory-Toyota International Centre for Economic and Related Disciplines, London School of Economics, January 1993.

[33] Juliet Rhys Williams, *op. cit.*, p.167.

complicate it with a work or participation test? Instead, given the hard reality that the BIs can never be more than partial, it makes more sense to restrict such tests to the non-BI part of the system. That is why Brandon Rhys Williams included work guarantee schemes, counselling and childcare provision among the responsibilities of his proposed Cash and Care departments (Figure 5.3).

Negative income tax (NIT)

Like participation income, NIT is on the borderlines of CI as defined in these pages (hence the dotted line in Figure 5.4). Yet it could become an essential weapon in the war against poverty. As originally proposed by Milton and Rose Friedman,[34] the basis of entitlement is legal residence; NI contributions can be abolished, everybody is entitled to the same degree of protection, and there are no earnings restrictions. Where NIT differs from other CI options is in its high benefit withdrawal rates (Appendix 5 C, below, pp.133, 135), its family-based assessment units and its greater administrative complexity. While other CI options take the year as the accounting period, NIT must be geared to respond within days or weeks. Also, because NIT produces the flattened net income curves associated with the poverty trap, it is either expensive to administer or open to abuse.

So long as full BI is unattainable, BI and NIT are best regarded as complementary, with partial BI helping to prevent poverty and NIT providing the safety net. This is close to the approach recommended by James Meade. The first slice of a really adequate social dividend, he wrote in 1972 referring to what would now be called Basic Income, should be subject to a special surcharge, making it a hybrid between a fully conditional and a fully unconditional benefit. This, he says, is a necessary but viable compromise between the disincentive effects if the whole amount is subject to a surcharge on the rate of income tax and the 'hideous expense' of no surcharge at all. Additionally, in order to avoid unnecessarily harsh disincentive effects, the threshold for positive income tax must always be above the break-even level at which the withdrawable benefits are fully phased out (a proviso that Treasury Ministers would do well to learn by heart).[35]

With these considerations in mind, the most productive approach is to think of BI and NIT as complementary policy instruments within

---

[34] Milton and Rose Friedman, *Capitalism and Freedom*, Chicago: University of Chicago Press, 1962; *Free to Choose*, Pelican, Harmondsworth: Penguin Books, 1981.

[35] James Meade, *op. cit.*, 1972 and 1993.

a single strategy: the challenge is to find the best balance between them. A dual system, with automated, universal, partial BIs and BI supplements operated by central government and an income-tested housing benefit/partial NIT operated locally, has much to commend it. If the income-tested components of this strategy included a participation test which encouraged positive discrimination, present problems could be greatly reduced, not just in the UK but in other 'post-industrial' economies as well.

6. PAYING FOR IT

To estimate the tax rate necessary to pay for a BI proposal, two methods are available. The *first* is to put the details of the proposal through a micro-simulation model, the *second* uses a formula which adds the costs of the proposed BIs to the costs of abolishing existing income tax and advance corporation tax; deducts savings on existing benefits; and divides the balance by the estimated new income tax base.[36] The difficulty is to estimate the tax base. The most reliable source is the Inland Revenue's Survey of Personal Incomes. Econometrics is unhelpful, because there are no reliable precedents to guide us.

Confusion about the cost of BI could at present hardly be worse. BI opponents exaggerate its cost. BI enthusiasts go the other way. Writing in 1985-86, I defined a 'full' BI as one-third average earnings (roughly £60 a week at that time) and showed that it would require a tax rate on all other income of 70 per cent or more.[37] Having demonstrated (as I thought) that 'full' BI is unsustainable, I turned to 'partial' BI, defined it as half the rate of supplementary benefit (or income support) for a married couple, and estimated a tax rate of between 35 and 40 per cent.[38] Today, a full BI worth one-third average earnings would be about £115 a week. Nobody is thinking in those terms, yet those earlier 'full' BI costings are still widely quoted as evidence that BI is either too expensive or useless. Indeed, the Liberal Democrats have just thrown out 16 years' commitment to BI on those very grounds.[39]

Another problem concerns non-personal income tax reliefs. All BI schemes abolish personal income tax allowances and most existing

---

[36] Hermione Parker, *op. cit.*, 1989, Appendix 1.

[37] Hermione Parker, *op. cit.*, 1989, pp.130-37.

[38] Hermione Parker, *op. cit.*, 1989, pp.238-40, 249-53, and 344-47.

[39] *Tax and Benefits*, Consultation Paper No. 10, Liberal Democrats, January 1994; *Citizen's Income Bulletin* No. 19, February 1995.

benefits, and there are strong arguments for getting rid of non-personal income tax reliefs as well, using the extra revenue to finance residence-based citizens' pensions at levels sufficient to remove the savings trap. Mortgage interest tax relief is already being phased out. In 1994-95 income tax reliefs for occupational and personal pensions and life insurance cost over £10,000 million in terms of revenue forgone (Appendix 6, below, p.136). The case for and against continuation of these reliefs is outside the terms of reference of this *Research Monograph*. It is, nevertheless, worth recording that a BI old-age supplement of £28 a week (from age 65) would cost roughly the same as the pension income tax relief and would lift some 1 million pensioner households out of income support, thereby helping to reduce the savings trap.[40] So the argument is really about priorities.

7. TRANSITIONAL BASIC INCOME

From the research of the past decade it is clear that basic income on a scale sufficient to replace income support cannot be implemented in a single go, partly because of the expense and partly because it would involve too many losers. One solution is to start by introducing small, transitional BIs (TBIs) of about £20 a week, reduce all NI benefits correspondingly, count the TBIs as a resource for income support and proceed towards a partial BI by increasing the TBIs annually in real terms until NI benefits, income support and family credit have all been replaced. The purpose of this proposal is to set in motion a self-generating cycle of falling benefit payrolls and increasing economic activity.

Starting in 1988, many TBI schemes have been costed and analysed using micro-simulation techniques, first at the London School of Economics and more recently at the Department of Applied Economics, University of Cambridge.[41] The year 1994-95 was a particularly difficult time to be costing any sort of CI. Britain's economy was emerging from its worst recession since the Second World War and there was a huge public sector borrowing requirement. Yet even then TBIs of £15 per week for adults and £12 for children would have been feasible. This option is called 'TBI 94'.

---

[40] *Source*: Polimod (for FES acknowledgement, see Author's Introduction, above, pp.14-15).

[41] The model used is called Polimod, written by Gerry Redmond, Holly Sutherland and Moira Wilson. See *POLIMOD: An Outline*, Microsimulation Unit Research Note MU/RN/5, Microsimulation Unit, Department of Applied Economics, University of Cambridge, 1994.

Transitional reform option: 'TBI 94'

The purpose of the 'TBI 94' simulation is not to produce a blueprint for reform, but to discover what could be achieved in a single budget, in a bad year, on a revenue-neutral basis, without requiring major legislative change, and to analyse its redistributive effects. Instead of personal income tax allowances, every adult is assumed to receive a TBI of £15 a week (£780 a year); instead of child benefit, every child receives a TBI of £12 a week (£624 a year); and there is a non-convertible tax credit of £5·72 a week on the first £22 a week of earned income.

It is assumed that the threshold for higher-rate income tax stays at £23,700, but applies as soon as the taxpayer's income reaches £23,700, instead of £23,700 plus income tax allowances and reliefs as at present. Private pension income tax reliefs remain but are restricted to 20 per cent. Mortgage interest tax relief is already restricted. The current 20 per cent band of income tax is abolished, and the April 1994 increase of 1 per cent in NI contribution is replaced by an increase of 1 per cent in the standard rate of income tax (in preparation for replacement of NI contributions by an integrated income tax). There is a new higher-rate tax band at 50 per cent on incomes above £65,000. The other changes in Table 5.2 are consequential.

TABLE 5.2: 'TBI 94'

1.	Adult TBIs of £15 a week replace all income tax allowances, except age allowance.
2.	Child TBIs of £12 a week replace child benefit.
3.	Earned-income tax credits introduced, worth a maximum of £5·72 a week.
4.	Abolition of 20% income tax band.
5.	Standard rate of income tax increased to 26%.
6.	NI contribution reduced to 9%.
7.	New 50% rate of income tax on taxable incomes above £65,000.
8.	Tax reliefs on superannuation and personal pension contributions restricted to 20%.
9.	TBIs deducted from existing NI benefits and counted as a resource for income support.
10.	All residual NI benefits and pensions become tax-free.
11.	Consequential changes to family credit, to ensure that low-income families do not lose out.
12.	Consequential changes to age allowance, to ensure that pensioners do not lose out.

The purpose of all stage-one TBI schemes is not to give claimants more income, but to change the basis of entitlement to benefit, so that it becomes a base on which they can build through paid work and saving instead of falling into a trap. In the case of families with children, this requires child BIs above the current levels of child benefit, but the extra expenditure is withdrawn from better-off families through the increased rates of income tax. Higher-rate taxpayers lose, as do most taxpayers at the cross-over into higher-rate tax. However, most single-wage families with children gain from the BI for the non-earning parent and the £12 child BIs, which compare with child benefit of £10·50 for first children and £8·25 for each subsequent child in 1994-95. Also of interest is the large number of families (about 80 per cent of all UK families) affected by the TBIs. Most gain, but just under one-third lose. Table 5.3 shows how the scheme would work for a low-wage couple with two children. *Their weekly gain is over £10 a week (nearly £530 a year) and they are lifted out of family credit.*

TABLE 5.3:
'TBI 94': single-wage couple with two children aged 4 and 6

Current position		£	'TBI 94'		£
	Earnings	200·00		Earnings	200·00
+	Child benefit	18·45	+	BIs	54·00
+	Family credit	4·46	+	Earned income tax credit	5·72
–	Income tax	23·94	–	Income tax	52·00
–	NI contribution	15·44	–	NI contribution	14·01
=	Net income	183·53	=	Net income	193·71
				Gain = £10·18	

Figure 5.5 shows average weekly gains (or losses) for each equivalised, net-income decile of UK families.[42] Each decile group contains approximately 3 million families (including single people). Those at the bottom gain an average of £10 a week (£520 a year), those at the top lose an average of £16·50 a week (£858 a year). Within those averages, 37 per cent of the bottom decile gain over £15 a week, 24 per cent gain between £5 and £15, and 2 per cent lose. One reason for the high level of gains is the high take-up of BI compared with means-tested benefits. In the top income decile, 31 per cent of families lose over £15 a week, 42 per cent lose between £5 and £15 a week and 16 per cent lose under £5.

---

[42] Equivalised net income is defined as family net income (before the policy change) divided by the following equivalence ratios: 1.00 for single people, 1.6 for couples, and 0.4 for each child.

FIGURE 5.5:
'TBI 94': Average weekly gains/losses, equivalent income deciles, all UK families

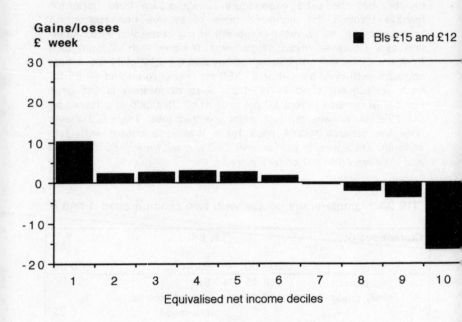

Source: Polimod (for FES acknowledgement, see Author's Introduction, above, pp.14-15).

'TBI 94' is revenue neutral. In Table 5.4 the tax increase of £24,000 million is an accounting illusion, because most people's BIs (like the tax allowances they would replace) are revenue forgone. It is only because the Treasury insists on counting BIs as public expenditure that income tax and public expenditure appear to go up. Notice also that the BIs are partly paid for by savings in existing benefits. Expenditure on income support goes down by £2,000 million. In distributional terms the main effects are three-fold: first, a transfer of net resources from top to bottom of the income distribution; second, a similar transfer from singles and couples without children to singles and couples with children (though lone-parent families do less well than two-parent families); third, gains to people who at present do not claim the benefits to which they are entitled, or for some reason have no entitlement.

TABLE 5.4:
'TBI 94' Costings, 1994-95

		£ billion	1994-95
Income tax and NI contributions	+		24·2
Adult BIs	−		33·6
Child BIs	−		7·7
Child benefit	+		6·0
NI benefit and statutory sick pay	+		8·8
Maternity benefits / maternity pay	+		0·2
Income support + IS housing benefit	+		2·0
Family credit	+		0·1
Housing benefit	+		0·0
Balance			0·0

Source: Polimod (for FES acknowledgement, see Author's Introduction, above, pp.14-15).

Transitional reform option: 'TBI 96'
The purpose of the 'TBI 96' option is to compare the redistributive and incentive effects of a 20 per cent standard rate of income tax with a stage-one TBI scheme. For it appears to be government policy to reduce the standard rate of income tax to 20 per cent before the next general election. The estimated revenue cost of this change (at 1994-95 prices and incomes) is £9,400 million.[43] If the same sum of money were used to start the ball rolling towards a partial BI system, it would be sufficient (again at 1994-95 prices and incomes) to finance TBIs of £20 a week for adults (age 16 and above) and £15·65 for children, with the first £22 of each person's weekly earnings tax-free.[44]

This simulation is included here in order to show that cutting the standard rate of income tax is a less effective way of increasing work incentives than convertible tax credits/basic incomes. In electoral terms a reduction of the standard rate to 20 per cent has immediate attractions, for it produces no losers and many gainers. However, it does virtually nothing to help families at risk of the various traps. Worse still, if its introduction required higher NI contributions, rents or council tax, or abolition of married couple's income tax allowance (as seems likely), the overall effect would be a further weakening of incentives and family life. By contrast, 'TBI 96' concentrates help at the bottom of the income distribution. At weekly earnings of £200, the gain from income tax at 20 per cent is a paltry 48 pence, compared with £27·48 from 'TBI 96' (Table 5.5).

---

[43] Using Polimod: see FES acknowledgement in Author's Introduction, above, pp.14-15.

[44] *Ibid.*

TABLE 5.5:
'TBI 96': Net Incomes Compared:
Single-wage married couple with two children,
weekly earnings £200

Existing System 1994-95	£	£ Income tax 20%	Integrated System 'TBI 96'	£
Earnings	200·00	200·00	Earnings	200·00
+ Child benefit	18·45	18·45	+ BIs	71·30
+ Family credit	4·46	1·14	+ EITC*	5·72
− Income tax	23·94	20·14	− Income tax	52·00
− NI contribution	15·44	15·44	− NI contribution	14·01
= Net Income	183·53	184·01	= Net Income	211·01

* EITC = Earned income tax credit.

Figure 5.6 shows the same pattern of income redistribution as Figure 5.5, except that the losses are smaller because £9,400 million has been 'spent' on the exercise. Cutting the standard rate of income tax (the diagonally striped columns) does not help families in the bottom decile at all and those in deciles (3) and (4) gain very little, after which the gains increase until they reach an average of £20·50 a week (over £1,000 a year) in the top decile (where they are not needed). About 50 per cent of families in decile (5) gain up to £5 a week (£260 a year), compared with 84 per cent of families in the top decile who gain more than £15 a week (£780 a year). By contrast 'TBI 96' produces descending gains with a slight hump in the middle of the income distribution, where large numbers of families with children are congregated. Gains averaging £14·44 a week (£750 a year) in the bottom decile compare with losses averaging £8·72 a week (£453 a year) in the top decile. Just under 58 per cent of families in the bottom decile gain over £15 a week, while 12 per cent in the top decile lose over £15 a week.

Trampoline or trap?
Cutting the standard rate of income tax to 20 per cent would at best leave work incentives at the bottom unaffected, whereas the incentive effects of a TBI depend on the BI amounts, which must be neither too large nor too small. For 'TBI 96', a child basic income of £15·65 was selected because that was the income support allowance for children aged under 11 in 1994-95. Getting rid of income support child allowances would drive a huge wedge in the unemployment trap. With TBIs of £20 for adults and £15·65 for children, income support (IS) entitlements fall dramatically. The IS

116

FIGURE 5.6:
'TBI 96' Compared with 20% Income Tax:
Average weekly gains/losses, equivalent income deciles,
all UK families

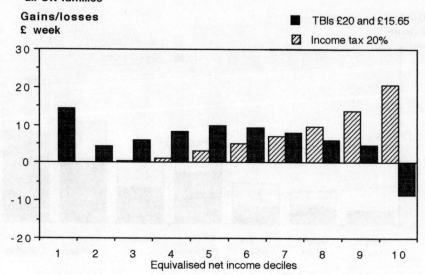

Source: Polimod (for FES acknowledgement, see Author's Introduction, above, pp.14-15).

entitlement for a couple with two children under 11 falls from £94·60 (plus child benefit) to £59 a week (plus the basic incomes).

In that case an unemployed couple has two choices. Either they can claim residual IS (with its earnings rules and invasion of privacy) or they can take whatever work is available, knowing that the first £22 earned by each parent is tax free and that residual family credit and housing benefit are still available.

In Figure 5.7, the total of each column represents the guaranteed income support allowances plus premia in 1994-95 for each of the selected family types. The black sections of the columns are the proportions of IS entitlements represented by the 'TBIs'. Because the TBIs count as a resource, IS payments are in most cases cut by over half. The exception is the IS allowance for a single person aged over 25, which has always been out of line.[45]

---

[45] Assuming that the income support allowances are supposed to provide an approximately equivalent living standard for all, if a single non-householder aged 25 plus needs £45.70, how can a pregnant mother produce a healthy baby on £26?

FIGURE 5.7:
Trampoline or Trap:
'TBI 96' Compared with Income Support

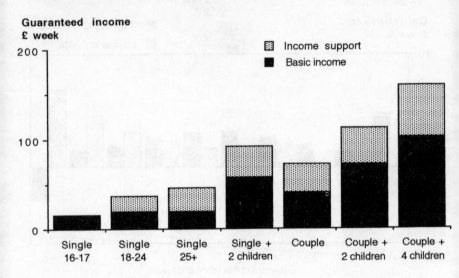

If a scheme like 'TBI 96' were introduced, no unemployed family would be worse off than before, because residual IS would remain, but more than half their benefit would become a trampoline instead of a trap. If they did not claim the IS due to them, they would not be subject to any earnings rule, the first £22 a week earned by each spouse would be tax-free, and residual family credit would remain available to them.

8. BRINGING THE TREASURY TO HEEL

The single biggest impediment to integration of the tax and benefit systems is the Treasury. By comparison with living standards generally, the BI amounts proposed in these pages are tiny. Their purpose is not to increase out-of-work living standards, but to change the nature of existing provisions in order to create platforms on which men and women at the edges of the labour market can build through their own efforts, without losing their privacy or being penalised by high tax and benefit-withdrawal rates. Why, therefore, does the Treasury object?

Writing for the journal of the Citizen's Income Trust, Christopher Monckton, who did research into basic income whilst a member of

Lady Thatcher's Policy Unit and to the dismay of the Treasury came out in favour of it, explained their attitude:

> 'At this point in our evaluation... a ludicrous snag appeared. The Treasury objected vigorously to any extension of "universal" benefits on grounds of cost. When we pointed out that one of our criteria was to ensure that the Exchequer did not lose by any proposed reform, we were told that any extension of universal benefits was bound to show a loss to the Exchequer, even if tax rates were raised to pay for it, because tax reliefs (which would be abolished...) do not count as public expenditure, while cash benefits (which would replace the tax reliefs) do. So public spending, as measured by the Treasury, would appear to soar...

> 'The futility of this argument becomes immediately apparent when one considers what happens when the State decides to withdraw an income tax relief and replace it with a cash benefit (as happened in 1979, when child benefit replaced child tax allowances). Let us suppose that Jane Taxpayer formerly received an income tax allowance worth £9 a week for her little Eustace. In reality, Jane was £9 a week richer, and the State £9 a week poorer than if Eustace had never been born. Yet in the Treasury's looking-glass world the State was no poorer even though Jane was richer.

> 'Since child tax allowances were abolished and replaced with direct cash benefits (child benefit), Jane has to pay, say, £9 a week more tax than she did when she got child tax allowance, but gets, say, £9 a week in child benefit instead. So she is no better off and no worse off. The Treasury, however, used not to count her child tax allowances as public spending, but does count her child benefit as public spending, so it declares itself £9 a week poorer as a result...

> 'Does all this matter? Yes it does, vitally, because national accounts prepared using this daft accounting principle are useless as a starting-point for policy formation.

> *'In particular, unless the Treasury is forced to mend its ways, it will always block the consideration of any universal benefit scheme, erroneously believing it to be in all circumstances unaffordable.'* [46]

---

[46] Christopher Monckton, *Universal benefit*, Citizen's Income Bulletin No. 16, July 1993, p.6 (Citizen's Income Study Centre).

PART SIX

Summary and Conclusions

Purpose of the Study

The purpose of this study has been:

- *First*, to analyse the effects of policy changes since 1979 on work incentives, voluntary savings and family life;

- *Second*, to find a way out of the present morass.

Without doubt the 1980s saw a big increase in work incentives for people at the top of the earnings distribution. Sadly, however, this improvement was marred by a deterioration at the bottom, where income tax cuts were offset by higher national insurance contributions, the falling away of non-means-tested family income support (especially married couple's income tax allowance and child benefit) and unprecedented increases in rents and local authority tax. A perverse by-product was the continuing erosion of differences in net spending power over a wide range of gross earnings, generally known as the poverty trap. Despite the 1988 social security reforms, the poverty trap and poverty plateau remain a major and growing cause of disincentive. Together the 'traps' identified in this study have produced a situation where for increasing numbers of people the only hope of self-advancement is through the underground or 'black' economy.

Incoherent Policies

Present contradictions are not due to increases in out-of-work benefits, which have fallen significantly in relation to gross earnings. The underlying cause is incoherent policy-making within and between the different government departments, together with the bland assumption that tax regardless of ability to pay ('TRAP') and escalating rents do not matter so long as those worst affected can claim means-tested rebates.

The main effect of a succession of cuts in national insurance benefits has been to increase dependence on income support (the UK's safety net of last resort), which is more damaging to self-reliance than unemployment benefit, sickness benefit or invalidity benefit, because it entails a means test as well as a work test, and takes the family instead of the individual as the assessment unit.

One effect is to reduce the incentive for wives to work when husbands become unemployed: at the latest count only 24 per cent of mothers with unemployed husbands were in paid work, compared with 68 per cent where the husband was in work.

Unwaged and single-wage families with children are disproportionately and increasingly at risk of work disincentives, because their out-of-work benefits are so much higher than their (in-work) child benefit and income tax allowances. When child benefit replaced family allowances and child tax allowances (in 1977), it appeared that the child additions payable with supplementary benefit might be subsumed within an increased child benefit. Instead, the gap between child benefit and the child allowances payable with income support has widened (Figure 4.8, above, p.84). Family credit is not the answer, because it leaves claimants with sometimes as little as 3 pence and often only 10 pence out of each extra £1 earned.

The Seven 'Traps'

Seven 'traps' stand out. They are the unemployment and invalidity traps, the poverty trap, the lone-parent trap, the part-time trap, the lack-of-skills trap and the savings trap. The part-time trap is a recent invention whereas the others were inherited. Most at risk of the traps are unskilled and semi-skilled workers, single-earner families with children, lone mothers, householders with mortgages, unemployed 'third-agers' in their fifties and early sixties, people with disabilities, and elderly people who scrimped and saved all their lives, only to find they are worse off than 'Joe Bloggs down the road who never did a proper day's work in his life'. They and others like them are the 'nearly poor' – whose earnings, savings or occupational pensions serve only to disqualify them from means-tested benefits.

In Britain today an unskilled family man in poor health has little chance of becoming financially independent. The more children he has and the higher his rent, the smaller are his chances. In 1985 an estimated 40 per cent of families with four or more children had no one at work, and those where someone was in work were in the upper end of the earnings distribution. By 1991, 45 per cent of families with four or more children had no workers. Today the figure is probably nearer 50 per cent.

Lone mothers are disproportionately at risk, because of their low earnings potential and high childcare costs. If the nub of the lone-parent trap in 1982 had been over-generous benefits, by now it would have gone. Instead, the number of lone parents on income support keeps rising. Kilos of evidence have been presented to the Treasury in support of childcare tax reliefs, but the response has been almost entirely negative. Even the £40 childcare disregard with family credit introduced in October 1994 is of little avail, for it is per family not per child and £40 compares with average weekly childcare charges in 1994 of £60 per child. The main result of the disregard is likely to be 'clustering' of earnings at levels where mothers can maximise their family credit and minimise their childcare costs, usually through part-time work.

This will add to Britain's burgeoning part-time trap. In April 1992, in an attempt to build bridges between unemployment and the labour market, the Department of Social Security reduced the hours threshold for family credit from 24 to 16 per week. Because of the high marginal deduction rates associated with family credit, this had the predictable effect of making part-time work more attractive than full-time work. By April 1994 the net gain for a couple with two children who increased their working hours from 16 to 40 per week (earning £3·75 an hour) was a miserable £5 (Figure 2.9, above, p.46). Since April 1995, in an effort to counter the part-time trap, families working 30 hours a week receive an extra £10 a week with their family credit – an implied hourly wage rate of only 70 pence.

A lack-of-skills 'trap' usually escapes attention. Despite increased emphasis on further education and training, students and trainees remain uniquely disqualified from income support on the grounds that they are not 'available for work'. Instead of making benefit conditional on participation in recognised training and study courses (as in Germany), the British system works in the opposite direction.

Scale of the Problem

Although it is difficult to estimate the number of people who succumb to moral hazard, figures published by the Institute for Fiscal Studies suggest that between 1979 and 1989 the number of pensioners at *risk* of disincentives fell by 10 per cent, while the number of working-age adults at risk approximately doubled (Appendix 2, below, p.129). Since 1989 the situation has worsened. By 1994 some 4 million working-age adults were on income support, compared with 1·4 million in 1979 and 2·9 million in 1989.

Families at Risk

Meanwhile, the traditional family, where the mother puts the children first and the father is the breadwinner, suffers from tax and benefit policies which undermine its financial independence during the crucial child-bearing and child-rearing years. In 1993, some 3½ million children were growing up in families where no one was in work, compared with 1 million in 1979 (Figure 3.2, above, p.56). In the under-five age group, nearly one-third were being reared in families receiving income support and a further 8 per cent in families receiving family credit – together accounting for almost 40 per cent of each pre-school cohort. Two-parent families are penalised in numerous ways. As regards family credit, they get *less benefit* than lone-parent families at the same level of earnings (Table 4.3, above, p.90), and the phasing out of married couple's income tax allowance will leave them paying the same amount of income tax as single people on the same income.

The Disaster of the Residual Welfare State and the Case for Change

Spending on social security is out of control. But the fastest-growing programmes are not pensions or child benefit, or even invalidity benefit. They are the so-called 'targeted' programmes: family credit (up 20-fold since 1979 at constant prices); income support for working-age claimants (up five-fold); and housing benefit (also up five-fold). Governments which pay people for not working and for being 'poor' end up with more people out of work and more 'poor'. Far from being a remedy for an already bad situation, the residual welfare state is turning into a disaster. But the main fault lies in the policy-makers, not the claimants.

If work-tested and means-tested benefits do more harm than good, it would be better to change the tax and benefit systems quickly rather than pretend the problem is under control. Otherwise, a continuing increase in the 'natural' rate of unemployment will have to be accepted or the unemployed will have to be directed into jobs. The question is not whether today's unemployed genuinely want to work, but about the price at which it is worthwhile for them to sell their labour and the speed with which they can find new jobs at the required wages. If each unemployed person takes on average twice as long as before to find an acceptable job, the unemployment count will double. Similarly, if living standards for skilled and unskilled labour converge – which happens with family credit – a lack of skilled workers and a surplus of unskilled labour will result and unemployment and skill shortages will exist simultaneously.

Perverse Effects – and Disposing of the 'Traps'

The problems identified in this *Research Monograph* will not be remedied by further reductions in benefits nor by further cuts in the standard rate of income tax, desirable though lower tax rates are.

One consequence of the present régime is that lower income tax rates may themselves have perverse effects. As explained in Section 4.3, they tend to raise the income levels at which some benefits (such as old-age pensions) are recouped by government. Moreover, because of the interaction of the tax and benefit systems, as at present constituted, reducing the standard rate may in practice swell government expenditure and increase state interference in people's affairs. Paradoxically, therefore, the scale of state activity could increase as a consequence of lower taxes. A precondition for effective tax-cutting is a fundamental overhaul of the present tax and benefit system.

To dispose of the 'traps' which now exist, the tax, social security, housing finance, education and training systems should be reformed as part of a single strategy in which consistent criteria are applied. In 1982, I suggested integration of the tax and benefit systems using either convertible tax credits (now known as basic incomes) or a negative income tax. Today, the most successful strategy is most likely to be a judicious combination of basic incomes (BIs) and income-tested benefits, the latter in the form of locally operated, income-tested housing benefit and/or negative income tax.

Basic incomes are fixed-amount tax credits that convert automatically into cash for citizens without the income to set against them, and thus become a base on which they can build through paid work and savings. A start could be made by converting all existing personal income tax allowances and child benefit into small, 'transitional' basic incomes (TBIs). The TBI 1996 proposal in this *Monograph* – £20 a week for adults and £15·65 for children – has an estimated cost (at 1994-95 prices and incomes) of £9,400 million, which by a curious chance is also the cost of reducing the standard rate of income tax to 20 per cent. The difference is that while a 20 per cent standard rate of income tax would redistribute income upwards, a £20 basic income would redistribute downwards. *With 'TBI 96' a single-wage couple with two children and weekly earnings of £200 would gain £27·50 a week and be lifted out of family credit, compared with a gain of only 48 pence if income tax were reduced to 20 per cent. The married couple's allowance would be replaced rather than abolished and the new system would not discriminate between men and women, nor between married and single.*

The Main Policy Implications

To summarise, there are three main policy implications of this study.

- *First*, that decisions which have an impact on household living standards, self-reliance and family solidarity should be taken together to ensure consistency – rather than separately as has generally been the case in the past.

- *Second*, that such decisions should be based on a careful examination of household living costs.

- *Third*, that government should make radical changes to the present régime, replacing all income tax allowances and child benefit by small 'unisex' basic incomes (or convertible tax credits).

Present-day Britain has, through a series of unintended consequences, arrived at a 'welfare' system which does not provide adequately for those in most need and yet contains severe disincentives to effort. Because it categorises people for benefit purposes, it is not surprising that a set of perverse incentives exists which induces people to try to move themselves into the categories in which they know benefits will be available. In other words, their enterprise is channelled away from productive activities into playing this system established by the state: they need to become 'victims' in order to establish 'rights' to benefit. Rather than condemn their behaviour, we should be urging politicians to make fundamental changes in a system which makes them behave in this way.

APPENDIX 1

PERCENTAGES OF EARNINGS TAKEN IN:
Income Tax, NI Contributions, Local Authority Rates / Council Tax, and Local Authority Rents, April 1979 and April 1994

	Single man	Single woman	Lone mother + 2 children	Single-wage couple	Single-wage couple + 2 children	Single-wage couple + 4 children
	%	%	%	%	%	%
Part 1. At average manual earnings [1]						
TOTALS						
1979	36·8	37·0	14·9	32·8	25·9	17·3
1994	41·3	44·6	31·1	39·4	35·7	29·8
OF WHICH:						
Income tax [2]						
1979	22·0	16·5	-8·5	18·0	9·4	0·8
1994	18·3	14·6	-2·8	15·7	9·2	3·3
NI contribution						
1979	6·5	6·5	6·5	6·5	6·5	6·5
1994	8·4	7·5	7·5	8·4	8·4	8·4
Rates/council tax [3]						
1979	2·5	4·2	5·1	2·5	3·0	3·0
1994	3·6	5·5	6·4	4·3	5·1	5·1
Rent						
1979	5·8	9·8	11·8	5·8	7·0	7·0
1994	11·0	17·0	20·0	11·0	13·0	13·0

[continued on p. 128]

	Single man	Single woman	Lone mother + 2 children	Single-wage couple	Single-wage couple + 2 children	Single-wage couple + 4 children
	%	%	%	%	%	%

Part 2. At two-thirds average manual earnings [1]

TOTALS

1979	36·9	37·2	6·1	30·9	20·5	7·6
1994	44·3	49·3	29·2	41·6	36·0	27·2

OF WHICH:
Income tax [2]

1979	18·0	9·9	-25·6	12·0	-1·0	-13·9
1994	14·9	9·3	-16·7	11·1	1·2	-7·6

NI contribution

1979	6·5	6·5	6·5	6·5	6·5	6·5
1994	7·6	6·2	6·2	7·6	7·6	7·6

Rates/council tax [3]

1979	3·7	6·2	7·6	3·7	4·5	4·5
1994	5·3	8·3	9·7	6·4	7·7	7·7

Rent

1979	8·7	14·6	17·6	8·7	10·5	10·5
1994	16·5	25·5	30·0	16·5	19·5	19·5

Source: DHSS / DSS Tax Benefit Model Tables, April 1979 and April 1994, but see Notes.

Notes: 1. Average manual earnings: April 1979: men £93, women £55; April 1994: men £281, women £182.
2. Child benefit and one-parent benefit are treated as a negative income tax.
3. To obtain comparability between the 1994 and 1979 figures, water rates at £3·40 a week have been added to the DSS council tax figures in 1994; and the four-child family in 1979 is assumed to occupy similar property to that of the two-child families.

APPENDIX 2

SCALE OF THE PROBLEM

Numbers of families, adults and persons at risk of the 'traps', 1979 and 1989: GB '000s

		FAMILIES		ADULTS		PERSONS	
		1979	1989	1979	1989	1979	1989
A.	**Receiving SB/IS:**						
	Pensioners	1,690	1,440	2,000	1,740	2,000	1,740
	Working age	1,110	2,480	1,370	2,890	2,350	4,890
B.	**Not receiving SB/IS, incomes below SB/IS**						
	Pensioners	1,130	1,110	1,430	1,280	1,450	1,280
	Working age	920	1,860	1,170	2,240	1,720	3,070
C.	**Not receiving SB/IS, incomes less than 40% above SB/IS**						
	Pensioners	3,040	2,820	4,090	3,750	4,140	3,750
	Working age	1,850	3,090	2,580	3,900	4,300	5,790
D.	**TOTAL AT RISK(A + C):**						
	Pensioners	4,730	4,260	6,090	5,490	6,140	5,490
	Working age	2,960	5,570	3,950	6,790	6,650	10,680
E.	**PERCENTAGE CHANGE**						
	Pensioners		-10%		-10%		-11%
	Working age		+88%		+72%		+61%

Source: Adapted from Christopher Giles and Steven Webb, *Poverty Statistics: A Guide for the Perplexed*, IFS Commentary No. 34, Institute for Fiscal Studies, January 1993, Tables 2, 3 and 5. Comparable figures for 1991-92, prepared for the House of Commons Social Security Select Committee, were not generally available when this Table was prepared.

Note: All the figures are after housing costs.

APPENDIX 3

INVALIDITY BENEFIT STATISTICS 1971 – 1992

Invalidity benefit spells,
Great Britain, commencing by period:

Period	Total spells commencing 000's
7 June 1971 – 3 June 1972	636
5 June 1972 – 2 June 1973	416
4 June 1973 – 1 June 1974	453
3 June 1974 – 31 May 1975	459
1 Sept 1975 – 6 June 1976	n/a
7 June 1976 – 4 June 1977	520
6 June 1977 – 3 June 1978	562
5 June 1978 – 2 June 1979	621
4 June 1979 – 31 May 1980	543
2 June 1980 – 30 May 1981	365
1 June 1981 – 29 May 1982	303
5 April 1982 – 2 April 1983	305
4 April 1983 – 31 March 1984	278
2 April 1984 – 30 March 1985	272
1 April 1985 – 5 April 1986	285
7 April 1986 – 4 April 1987	284
6 April 1987 – 2 April 1988	282
4 April 1988 – 1 April 1989	280
3 April 1989 – 31 March 1990	284
2 April 1990 – 30 March 1991	288
1 April 1991 – 4 April 1992	323

Source: Hansard, Written Answer, 1 February 1994, col. 690.

APPENDIX 4

SAMPLE FAMILY BUDGET UNIT BUDGETS

October 1993 prices, rented housing

HOUSEHOLDS	A	B	C	D	E	F
	£ week	£ week	£ week	£ week	£ week	£ week
Housing[1]	44·13	34·17	31·20	43·82	43·82	43·82
Council tax[1]	5·79	4·96	6·62	7·72	7·72	5·79
Fuel	8·47	5·71	7·11	14·60	14·90	13·18
Food	19·00	25·54	39·56	58·14	69·20	43·17
Alcohol	5·17	8·10	13·89	13·89	13·89	5·79
Tobacco	0·00	0·00	0·00	0·00	0·00	0·00
Clothing	6·51	7·03	15·05	29·88	31·79	22·90
Personal care	3·41	3·81	8·98	11·10	13·92	7·81
Household goods[2]	10·87	9·06	13·90	24·50	25·42	22·92
Household services[3]	3·44	4·22	6·04	6·55	8·26	4·54
Motoring [4]	0·00	35·52	35·56	38·45	37·90	36·06
Fares etc.	4·97	3·34	5·57	10·92	13·60	5·31
Leisure goods [5]	6·68	6·31	8·65	15·69	16·06	15·45
Leisure services[6]	7·15	11·09	21·12	18·13	23·21	12·22
Childcare	0·00	0·00	0·00	27·81	6·82	67·24
Trade union dues	0·00	1·29	2·57	1·93	1·95	1·25
Pets	3·34	0·00	3·34	5·77	5·77	5·77
EXPENDITURE TOTALS	128·93	160·16	219·16	328·90	334·23	313·22
+ INCOME TAX AND NIC	12·82	47·83	32·48	82·33	82·05	101·70
− CHILD BENEFIT	0·00	0·00	0·00	18·10	18·10	24·15
= WEEKLY EARNINGS REQUIRED	141·75	207·99	251·64	393·13	398·18	390·77
ANNUAL EARNINGS REQUIRED £	7,370	10,815	13,085	20,440	20,705	20,320

[continued on page 132]

KEY:

    A: Single woman pensioner.

    B: Single man.

    C: Married couple, wife earns £95 a week.

    D: Couple with boy aged 10 and girl aged 4, wife earns £65 a week.

    E: Couple with girl aged 16 and boy aged 10, wife earns £100 a week.

    F: Lone mother with two children, boy aged 10, girl aged 4, mother works full-time.

NOTES:

1. Actual York rents, council tax, water and sewerage charges in Oct 93.
2. Costs of durables are spread over product lifetimes.
3. Includes telephone and postage.
4. Includes travel to work in a second-hand car.
5. Includes daily newspaper, magazines, books and television.
6. Includes health-promoting sports activities and a self-catering or package annual holiday.

METHOD: First the component budgets for housing, fuel, food, clothing, personal care, household goods and services, transport and leisure goods and services are prepared by specialists in each field, taking into account need as well as consumer preferences. Then the component budgets are added together, and grossed up for income tax and NI contribution.

Source: Family Budget Unit Ltd, King's College London, Department of Nutrition and Dietetics, London W8 7AH.

APPENDIX 5

HOW TO PREVENT POVERTY AND ENCOURAGE WEALTH CREATION

The diagrams on page 135 compare the effects of four tax-benefit reform options on the net incomes and income tax liabilities of a single person. The 45° line shows the relationship between gross income (GY) and net income (NY), assuming no tax or cash transfers. Point G is the income guarantee level (where there is one), and the aim is to raise point G to the poverty level (P), whilst simultaneously avoiding excessive tax increases and reducing the number of families at risk of work and other disincentives. None of the options is costed, nor do they take into account the long-term effects of the proposal.

Option A shows the existing system. The line OAB shows the relationship between gross and net income under the existing system, point A being the tax break-even point at which tax starts to be paid. Net income rises along the 45° degree line until the personal tax allowance is used up, after which tax cuts in at an assumed 35 pence in the £ (to take account of NI contribution).

Option B assumes the introduction of a basic income large enough to 'prevent poverty' and a constant tax rate of 70 per cent. Point G goes up to the poverty line, the line GAB shows the new relationship between gross income and net income, and point A (the tax-break-even level) moves over to the right, indicating benefit leakage to people who do not need it, in the triangle GAC.

Option C assumes the introduction of a negative income tax large enough to 'prevent poverty' (on the same definition as before). Point G is again at the poverty line but this time the line GAB is kinked, because the rate of benefit withdrawal below the tax break-even level (point A) is higher than the rate of positive tax above it. The size of the GAC triangle is much smaller than with a full basic income. However, all those people in the GAO triangle are subject to benefit withdrawal rates of over 90 per cent.

Option D (partial basic income) removes the problem of excessive tax associated with full basic income, reduces the poverty gap without any poverty trap effects, but leaves much poverty unattended to. Point G is well below the poverty line.

[continued on p.134]

Since none of these solutions, on its own, combines poverty prevention with wealth creation, a compromise solution has to be found.

Option E (Basic Income Guarantee) is one such compromise. It has three main ingredients:

- A 'partial' basic income sufficient for non-householders to live on.
- A tax discount on the first slice of 'own' income.
- An income-tested housing benefit.

With this solution the guarantee level (G) is at the poverty line. For non-householders the tax schedule (TDAB) becomes gently progressive. For low-income householders it is kinked (PGAB), as with negative income tax, but the number of people affected is far fewer, due to the partial BI and the tax discount.

[Appendix 5 continued on p. 135]

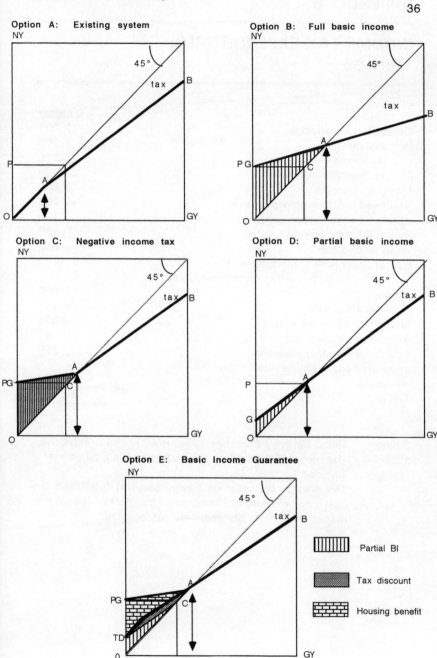

Option A: Existing system

Option B: Full basic income

Option C: Negative income tax

Option D: Partial basic income

Option E: Basic Income Guarantee

Partial BI

Tax discount

Housing benefit

APPENDIX 6

INCOME TAX EXPENDITURES, 1994-95

	£ million
Occupational pensions	7,200
Personal pensions	1,900
Life assurance	170
Private medical insurance	95
Mortgage interest	3,500
Approved profit sharing schemes	105
Approved share option schemes	180
Personal Equity Plans	180
Profit related pay	500
Half of Class 4 NI contributions	130
First £30,000 of payments on termination of employment	1,000
Personal allowance	25,900
Married couple's allowance	3,500
Age-related allowances	750
Additional personal allowance	250
Invalidity benefit and severe disablement allowance	800
TOTAL	**46,160**

Source: *Inland Revenue Statistics 1994*, HMSO, 1994, Table 1.6.
Note: The cost of tax relief for employers' contributions is included.
The cost of tax relief on capital gains of funds and the cost of exempting lump-sum payments related to retirement annuity contracts are not included.

Glossary of Abbreviations and Technical Terms and Short Guide to Social Security Benefits

BI Basic income
BIG   Basic Income Guarantee
CI Citizen's income
DHSS Department of Health and Social Security
DSS   Department of Social Security
FIS Family income supplement
FC Family credit
IS Income support
IVB   Invalidity benefit
MCA   Married couple's allowance (income tax)
MBA   Modest-but-adequate (living standard)
NI National insurance
NIT   Negative income tax
PAYE Pay as you earn (income tax)
SB Supplementary benefit
TBI Transitional basic income
TRAP Tax regardless of ability to pay

1. Net income, net spending power and replacement ratios

Net income: earnings less income tax and NI contribution, plus child benefit where appropriate.

Net spending power: earnings less income tax, NI contribution, local authority tax, rent or mortgage and work expenses, plus child benefit and means-tested benefits.

Replacement ratio: income received when out of work as a proportion of income from employment (either previous or prospective).

Net income replacement ratio: net income when out of work as a proportion of net income from employment (previous or prospective).

Net spending power replacement ratio: net spending power out of work as a proportion of net spending power when in employment (previous or prospective). This the ratio that matters most.

2. The 'Traps'

Unemployment, invalidity and income support traps: the erosion of differentials between living standards in and out of work, as a result of which people are encouraged to stay out of work for longer than is strictly necessary, to work spasmodically or not at all.

Poverty trap: the high marginal deduction rates which result from charging income tax, NI contribution and council tax on earnings below the recognised poverty levels *and at the same time as* means-tested benefits are being withdrawn.

Poverty plateau: the levelling of spending power differentials over a wide band of gross earnings, which results from charging income tax, NI contribution and council tax *at the same time as* means-tested benefits are being withdrawn.

Lone-parent trap: the combination of poverty trap and unemployment trap effects to which lone parents are particularly susceptible, due to their low earnings potential and high childcare costs.

Part-time trap: the erosion of spending power differentials between full-time and part-time work, caused by reducing the hours threshold for eligibility to family credit to 16 hours of work per week.

Lack of skills trap: imbalance between demand for and supply of skilled labour caused by exclusion of most students and trainees from any sort of minimum income guarantee.

Savings trap: the levelling of spending power differentials across a wide band of pensioner incomes, as a result of which small savings and small occupational or personal pensions are not worthwhile.

3. Main social security benefits

The following is a brief guide:

(1) NATIONAL INSURANCE BENEFITS: Entitlement depends on work status and/or age, contribution record and family circumstances. NI benefits are not means-tested, but with the exception of retirement pension they are subject to strict earnings rules. The assessment unit is the individual contributor, but adult and child dependency additions may also be payable. Weekly flat-rate amounts payable for the main benefits are shown below. Earnings-related supplements may also be payable. In April 1995 NI sickness and invalidity benefits (IVB) were replaced by incapacity benefit (ICB), a new medical test was introduced and the lower rate of statutory sick pay was abolished. Short-term ICB is paid at a lower rate for the first six months and a higher rate for the second six months. The lower rate equates to former NI sickness benefit, the higher rate is less than former IVB. Long-term ICB equates to the basic rate of IVB, but entitlement begins after twelve month of incapacity instead of six months previously. Earnings-related supplements have been abolished for new ICB claimants. ICB counts as part of taxable income after 28 weeks of incapacity.[1]

---

[1]   For an introduction to the complexities of UK social security benefits, see *Social Security Statistics* (DSS); *Rights Guides to Non-Means-Tested*

Main NI Benefits	1994	1995
	£ week	£ week
Unemployment benefit	45.45	46.45
Adult dependent	28.05	28.65
Child dependent	0.00	0.00
TOTAL FOR COUPLE + 2 CHILDREN	73.50	75.10
plus child benefit	18.45	18.85
TOTAL	92.00	93.95
Statutory sick pay		
Higher rate	52.50	
Lower rate	47.80	
Standard rate		52.50
(No dependency additions)		
Sickness benefit/short-term ICB (lower rate)	43.45	44.40
Adult dependent	26.90	27.50
Child dependent	0.00	0.00
TOTAL FOR COUPLE + 2 CHILDREN	70.35	71.90
plus child benefit	18.45	18.85
TOTAL	88.80	90.75
Short-term ICB (higher rate)		52.50
Adult dependent		27.50
Child dependent		11.05
TOTAL FOR COUPLE + 2 CHILDREN		100.90
plus child benefit		18.85
TOTAL		119.75
Invalidity benefit/long-term ICB	57.60	58.85
Adult dependent	34.50	35.25
Child dependent	11.00	11.05
TOTAL FOR COUPLE + 2 CHILDREN	112.90	115.00
plus child benefit	18.45	18.85
TOTAL	131.35	133.85

(2) INCOME SUPPORT (IS): IS replaced supplementary benefit in 1988. IS is non-contributory but means-tested. Claimants must be out of work but available for work or excused from work, e.g. on account of incapacity or lone parenthood. The adult scale rates count as part of taxable income. Families receiving IS get their council tax and 'reasonable' rent paid in full, free school meals, free

Benefits, and *National Welfare Benefits Handbooks* (Child Poverty Action Group).

welfare milk and free prescriptions, but most of the extras available with former supplementary benefit have been removed. Mortgage interest remains payable, but only after prescribed periods and within prescribed ceilings. Premiums are sometimes payable in addition to the personal allowances. Thus a lone mother gets personal allowances for herself and each of her children, plus a family premium and a lone-parent premium. IS is subject to a capital limit of £8,000.

Income Support	1994	1995
	£ week	£ week
Personal Allowances		
Single		
under 18 - usual rate	27.50	28.00
18 to 24	36.15	36.80
25 or over	45.70	46.50
Lone parent (18 or over)	45.70	46.50
Couple (one or both 18 or over)	71.70	73.00
Dependent children		
under 11	15.65	15.95
11 to 15	23.00	23.40
16 to 17	27.50	27.50
18	36.15	36.80
Premiums		
Family	9.65	10.25
Lone Parent	4.90	5.20
Pensioner	age-related	
Disability	various	
Social Fund Payments		
Maternity expenses	100.00	100.00
Cold weather payments	7.00	8.50
TOTAL FOR COUPLE + 2 CHILDREN		
UNDER 11	94.60	96.30
plus child benefit	18.45	18.85
TOTAL	113.05	115.15

Plus rent and council tax in full, free school meals, free welfare milk, and other passport benefits.

(3) CHILD BENEFIT AND ONE-PARENT BENEFIT: Non-contributory, non-means-tested and tax-free. Child benefit was phased in between 1977 and 1979 as a replacement for former family allowances and child tax allowances. One-parent benefit also took effect from April 1977. The following amounts are payable weekly in respect of

children aged under 16, or aged 16 to 19 but still in full-time non-advanced education:

Child Benefit	1994	1995
	£ week	£ week
Child benefit (first or only children)	10.20	10.40
Child benefit (each subsequent child)	8.25	8.45
One-parent benefit (first or only child in each one-parent family)	6.15	6.30

(4) FAMILY CREDIT (FC): FC replaced family income supplement (FIS) in April 1988. Unlike FIS, which was restricted to families working at least 30 hours a week (24 hours for lone parents), FC is payable to families working at least 16 hours a week (on average). In 1994-95 the maximum FC amounts payable were as shown in the table. Family credit is calculated using the following formula:

FC = (Adult Credit + Child Credits) − (taper x (excess [if any] of Net Income over Applicable Amount))

In 1994-95 the withdrawal rate (or taper) was 70% (it still is), and the applicable amount was £71.40. The 1994-95 rates of credit are shown below:

Family Credit	1994
	£ week
Credit for single parent or couple	44.00
Credit for child aged: under 11	11.15
11 to 15	18.45
16 to 17	23.00
18	32.10

Since October 1994 up to £40 of child-care costs can be offset against earnings in certain cases. Since April 1995 families who work 30 hours a week or more get an extra £10.

(5) HOUSING BENEFIT AND COUNCIL TAX BENEFIT: The amount of housing benefit payable depends on 'eligible' rent, income, deductions for non-dependants living in the household and the 'applicable amount'. Eligible rent is the amount of rent which can be met by housing benefit, it may not be the actual amount paid, for instance if the amount of rent payable is unreasonably high or the accommodation over-large. Eligible rent and council tax are payable in full with income support, but working claimants get at best a rebate. Income for housing benefit purposes means income after income tax and NI contributions and certain disregards (e.g. the first £15 of maintenance). The 'applicable amount' consists of a personal

allowance depending on family composition, together with premiums for disability, pensioners, lone parents, children and so forth.

Cumulative deductions from each £1 of gross earnings are as shown below:

Cumulative Deductions	Family	Single/couple no children
Income tax @ 20%	20p	20p
National Insurance	10p	10p
Net Earnings	70p	70p
Family Credit (at 70% of 70p)	49p	nil
Net balance	21p	70p
Housing benefit (@ 65%)	14p	45.5p
Council Tax benefit	4p	14p
Net Disposable Income	3p	10.5p

Source: S. Wilcox, *The Costs of Higher Rents*, York: Joseph Rowntree Foundation, Housing Finance Review 1994/95.

4. Income tax, technical terms

Tax Threshold: The level of earnings which may be received before liability to tax arises.

Tax-free Income: Total income (earnings plus benefit) which may be received before liability to tax arises.

Tax Break-even Point: The level of income at which income tax paid equals state benefits received.

Tax Allowance: An allowance against taxable income, the value of which (to the taxpayer) is a function of his or her marginal tax rate. In 1994-95, for example, the personal allowance of £3,445 was worth £861 a year (£16·56 a week) to standard-rate taxpayers, compared with £1,378 a year (£26·50 a week) to higher-rate taxpayers and nothing at all to people without the income to set against it. The main personal income tax allowances and bands of taxable income in 1994-95 and 1995-96 are shown below:

Income Tax Allowances	1994	1995
	£ year	£ year
Personal allowances	3,445	3,525
Married couple's allowance)		
Additional personal allowance)	1,720	1,720
Widow's bereavement allowance)		
For people aged 65-74		
personal allowance	4,200	4,630
married couple's allowance	2,665	2,995
For people aged 75 or over		
personal allowance	4,370	4,800
married couple's allowance	2,705	3,035
Income limit for age-related allowances	14,200	14,600

Taxable income: Income that is reckonable for tax. Child benefit, being tax-free, does not count as part of taxable income, but most social security benefits do. This need not mean that low-income families pay income tax on their NI benefits. By keeping income tax allowances above benefit levels this can be avoided. Child benefit is tax-free because there are no child tax allowances to set against it.

Bands of taxable income:

	1994 £ year	1995 £ year
Lower rate: 20%	0-3,000	0-3,200
Basic rate: 25%	3,001-23,700	3,200-24,300
Higher rate: 40%	over 23,700	over 24,300

Tax credits: Unlike tax allowances, which vary in value according to the marginal tax rate of the taxpayer, tax credits are fixed-amount, lump sum deductions against income tax. For example, what remains of married couple's allowance is now a tax credit worth 15 per cent of £1720 (i.e. £258 in 1995-96).

Convertible tax credits/basic incomes: Some tax credits convert into cash benefits if the taxpayer does not have the income to set against them. Child benefit is a convertible tax credit/basic income for families with children. In the days of child tax allowances, some families earned too little to be able to use up their child tax allowances. Today child benefit is at the same flat rates for everyone.

Basic income guarantee ('BIG'): This is a modified basic income (BI) option. Every legal resident, including children, receives an age-related, 'partial' basic income, defined as not enough to live on. Additionally, selective 'demogrant' groups (e.g. old age pensioners) receive BI supplement. The partial BIs are sufficient to meet all basic needs except housing. For those on low incomes there is also an income-tested housing benefit, operated locally by newly appointed 'Cash-and-Care' departments. (See above, Part 5, pp.99-102.)

Negative income tax : Families with incomes below a predetermined poverty line receive negative income tax (NIT) while those with incomes above the poverty line pay positive income tax. Usually the NIT is phased out at benefit withdrawal rates that are higher than the rates of positive income tax above the poverty line.

5. Budget Standards

These are specified baskets of goods and services which, when priced, can represent predefined living standards. Budget standards methodology was pioneered by Seebohm Rowntree in his study of poverty in York (1901). Today, as a result of computer technology, it is easier to produce and has greater potential, but the Department of Social Security (DSS) rejects it on the grounds that it is 'unscientific'. It has, however, been reintroduced by the *Family Budget Unit,* based initially at the University of York and now at the Department of Nutrition and Dietetics, King's College, London. Each basket of goods has the following components: housing, fuel, food, clothing, household goods and services, personal care, transport, leisure goods and services, council tax, NI contributions and income tax. The contents of each 'basket' are selected using a combination of normative (expert) judgements about how much people need and empirical analysis of consumer behaviour. The DSS relies entirely on empirical analysis. To date, the *Family Budget Unit* has devised budgets for seven household types. In theory, it is possible to cost a range of living standards, but the living standards generally regarded as most valuable are low-cost or poverty (below which good health may be at risk) and modest-but-adequate (MBA), defined as above the requirements of survival and decency, but well below luxury as generally understood. To date, the *Family Budget Unit* has concentrated on the MBA standard. At that level (roughly twice the poverty line) it is possible to purchase a small flat or house, run a second-hand car, take a short annual holiday and avoid debt problems.

6. Equivalence ratios

These show the extent to which household expenditure has to be increased (or diminished) to yield the same standard of living for households of different sizes and composition. Taking a single householder as the reference point, with a scale of 1·00, and assuming living costs at the modest-but-adequate level of £160 a week, the equivalence ratio for a married couple, assuming living costs of £220 becomes:

$$\frac{220}{160} \times 100 = 138$$

For families with children, the equivalence ratios are higher. With the single householder as the reference point, and assuming that a couple with 2 children aged 4 and 10 need £330 a week to reach the MBA living standard, their equivalence ratio becomes 206. In other words, their net income (after adding child benefit and deducting tax) needs to be over twice as much as the net income of a single householder:

$$\frac{330}{160} \times 100 = 206.$$

7. Citizen's Income

A citizen's income (CI) is a guaranteed income granted on the basis of citizenship or legal residence. In Britain the only existing example is child benefit, but the residence-based pensions payable in Scandinavia, Holland and Canada come close to CIs for old age. The main CI varieties are: basic income (*cf.* convertible tax credits), social dividend, participation income and negative income tax. CI protagonists start from the premise that economic and social progress depend on unpaid as well as paid work, and that societies which restrict benefit entitlement to paid workers (or former paid workers) risk chronic unemployment and social disintegration.

Bibliography

Atkinson, A.B. and J. Micklewright, 'Turning the Screw: Benefits for the Unemployed', in A.B. Atkinson, *Poverty and Social Security*, Harvester Wheatsheaf, 1989.

Atkinson, A.B., *Beveridge, The National Minimum, and its Future in a European Context*, Discussion Paper WSP / 85, STICERD, London School of Economics, 1993.

Beveridge, W., *Social Insurance and Allied Services*, Cmd. 6405, London: HMSO, 1942.

Beveridge, W., *Voluntary Action*, London: George Allen & Unwin, 1948.

Bradshaw, J. (ed.), *Household Budgets and Living Standards*, York: Joseph Rowntree Foundation, 1993.

Bradshaw, J. (ed.), *Budget Standards for the United Kingdom*, Aldershot: Avebury, 1993.

Brittan, S., and S. Webb, *Beyond the Welfare State: An Examination of Basic Incomes in a Market Economy*, The David Hume Institute, Aberdeen University Press, 1990.

Dean, H., and P. Taylor-Gooby, *Dependency Culture*, Harvester Wheatsheaf, 1992.

Cassels, J., *Britain's Real Skill Shortage*, London: Policy Studies Institute, 1990.

Commission on Social Justice, *Social Justice: Strategies for National Renewal*, London: Vintage, 1994.

Department of Social Security, *The Growth of Social Security*, London: HMSO, 1994.

Department of Social Security, *The Government's Expenditure Plans, 1994-95 to 1996-97*, Cm. 2513, London: HMSO, 1994.

Department of Social Security, *Households below Average Income, A Statistical Analysis, 1979 – 1991/92*, London: HMSO, 1994.

Evans, M., D. Piachaud, H. Sutherland, *Designed for the Poor – Poorer by Design? The Effects of the 1986 Social Security Act on Family Incomes*, Discussion Paper WSP / 105, Welfare State Programme, STICERD, London School of Economics, 1994.

Evason, E., and R. Woods, 'Poverty, Deregulation of the Labour Market and Benefit Fraud', *Social Policy & Administration*, Vol. 29, No. 1, 1995.

Family Budget Unit, *Introducing the Work of the Family Budget Unit*, King's College London, Department of Nutrition and Dietetics, 1994.

Friedman, M., and R. Friedman, *Capitalism and Freedom*, University of Chicago Press, 1962; *Free to Choose*, Pelican, 1981.

Giles, C., and S. Webb, *Poverty Statistics: A Guide for the Perplexed*, IFS Commentary No. 34, Institute for Fiscal Studies, London, January 1993.

Gregg, P., and J. Wadsworth, *More Work in Fewer Households*, National Institute for Economic and Social Research Discussion Paper 72, NIESR, London, 1994.

Handy, C., *The Age of Unreason*, London: Hutchinson, 1989, Arrow, 1990.

Howell, R., *Why Work? A Challenge to the Chancellor* ; *Why Work? A radical solution*, Conservative Political Centre, 1976 and 1981.

Jordan, B., S. James, H. Kay, and M Redley, *Trapped in Poverty: Labour-Market Decisions in Low-Income Households*, London: Routledge, 1992.

Keep, E., and K. Mayhew, 'Education, Workforce Training and Economic Performance in Britain', in C. Buechtemann and D. Soloff (eds.), *Human Capital Investments and Economic Performance*, Sage, 1994.

Marsh, A., and S. McKay, *Families, Work and Benefits*, Policy Studies Institute, London, 1993; and 'Families, Work and the Use of Childcare', *Employment Gazette*, August 1993.

Meade, J.E., 'Poverty and the Welfare State', *Oxford Economic Papers*, Vol. 24, No. 3, Oxford: Clarendon Press, 1972.

Meade, J.E., *Liberty, Equality and Efficiency*, London: Macmillan, 1993.

Parker, H., *The Moral Hazard of Social Benefits*, IEA Research Monograph No. 37, London: Institute of Economic Affairs, 1982.

Parker, H., *Action on Welfare*, London: Social Affairs Unit, 1984.

Parker, H. (ed.), *Basic Income and the Labour Market*, Citizen's Income Study Centre, c/o London School of Economics, 1991.

Parker, H. (ed.), *Citizen's Income and Women*, Citizen's Income Study Centre, c/o London School of Economics, 1992.

Rathbone, E., *The Disinherited Family*, 1924; *Family Allowances*, London: Allen and Unwin, 1949.

Rhys Williams, B. (ed. H. Parker), *Stepping Stones to Independence: National Insurance after 1990*, Aberdeen University Press, 1989.

Rhys Williams, J., *Something To Look Forward To: A Suggestion for a New Social Contract*, Cardiff: Western Mail and Echo Limited, August 1942, and London: Macdonald & Co., 1943.

Sly, F., 'Mothers in the Labour Market', *Employment Gazette*, November 1994.

Social Security Advisory Committee, *The Review of Social Security: Paper 1, In work – out of work: The rôle of incentives in the benefits system*, July 1994; Paper 3, *Housing Benefit*, May 1995.

Titmuss, R.M., 'The Social Division of Welfare', in *Essays on the Welfare State*, London: Allen & Unwin, 1958.

Treasury, *The Reform of Personal Taxation*, Green Paper, Cmnd. 9756, London: HMSO, 1986.

Treasury and DHSS, *Proposals for a Tax-Credit System*, Green Paper, Cmnd. 5116, London: HMSO, 1972.

ECONOMIC AFFAIRS
The journal of the IEA

Autumn 1995
Monetary Policy Issue

Main Articles
(edited by Professor Geoffrey E. Wood)

Individual issue £2.50

Annual subscriptions:

UK & Europe: £15.00 (Institution); £10.00 (Individual);

**Rest of the World: £20.00/$35.00 (Surface);
£30.00/$50.00 (Air)**

Please apply to:

**Institute of Economic Affairs
2 Lord North Street, London SW1P 3LB**

Telephone: 0171-799 3745: Fax: 0171-799 2137

Utility Regulation: Challenge and Response

Eleven years after the first utility privatisation, the agenda has moved from whether privatisation will do better than its state predecessor to the question of how to do better with privatisation. The future of regulation seems very uncertain.

The stakeholders – consumers, politicians, the companies themselves and their shareholders – are increasingly critical. Regulatory processes have borne the brunt of criticism.

Conflicting remedies are suggested for the problems which have arisen. Should there be more competition? Should regulators' powers be increased and perhaps widened? Should some of their Offices be amalgamated? Should the respective powers of the Office of Fair Trading and the Monopolies and Mergers Commission be reconsidered? Should government become more involved in regulation?

Each year the IEA, in association with the London Business School, publishes a volume of Readings which provides an up-to-date assessment of the state of utility regulation. In this, the latest in the series, the regulators themselves discuss the problems they face and leading commentators assess the regulators' contributions. The result is a wealth of detail about utility regulation in Britain – where it is now and where it may be going.

Contents

ISBN: 0-255 36349-4   IEA Readings 42

£15.00

The Institute of Economic Affairs
2 Lord North Street, Westminster
London SW1P 3LB
Telephone: 0171-799 3745
Fax: 0171-799 2137